# MAKING REVISION MATTER

## JANET ANGELILLO

■SCHOLASTIC

NEW YORK • TORONTO • LONDON • AUCKLAND • SYDNEY
MEXICO CITY • NEW DELHI • HONG KONG • BUENOS AIRES

# DEDICATION

*To Carl Anderson, who came to my classroom*
*and revised my teaching life*

## CREDITS

Page 47: Reprinted with the permission of Atheneum Books for Young Readers, an imprint of Simon & Schuster Children's Publishing Division, from *Night in the Country* by Cynthia Rylant. Text copyright © 1986 by Cynthia Rylant.

Page 55: Cover image from *Come On, Rain!* by Karen Hesse, illustrated by Jon Muth. Illustration copyright © 1999 by John Muth. Reprinted by permission of Scholastic Inc.

Page 102: Used by permission of HarperCollins Publishers from *Wolves* copyright © 1993 by Seymour Simon.

Cover design by Jason Robinson
Interior design by Maria Lilja
Cover photo: © 2002 by Royalty-Free/CORBIS
Interior photos by James Levin

ISBN: 0-439-49156-8

© 2005 by Janet Angelillo
All rights reserved. Published by Scholastic Inc.
Printed in the U.S.A.

2 3 4 5 6 7 8 9 10  23  09 08 07 06 05

# TABLE OF CONTENTS

# ACKNOWLEDGMENTS

Thanks to my colleagues, whose thinking supports mine every day: Carl Anderson, Shirley McPhillips, Katie Ray, and Isoke Nia. And thanks always to Lucy Calkins and the members of the Teachers College Reading and Writing Project. You are all always with me.

Thanks to the teachers and administrators, whose work in schools matters more than anything: Mary Ellyn Lehner and Stephanie Rypka of Bethel Middle School; Kerry Moscato, Amy Condit, Deborah Scofield, and Raina Kor of Irvington Middle School; Lisa Schofield, Judy Nadler, Joan Snell, Philip Levine, and Dolores Garcia-Blocker of Main Street School in Irvington; Barbara Rosenblum and Anouk Weiss of PS 6 in New York City; Connie Wu, Karen Perepeluk, and Maria Iams of PS 59 in New York City; Helen Jurios of PS 206 in Queens; Cheryl Lewis of Ridgefield, Connecticut; Tina Colangelo, Rebecca Mikus, and Cheryl Dwyer of Canton Intermediate School; Susan VanBlarcom, Jacqueline Heibert, and Laura Hill of Crofton House School; Tina Dolan and Barbara Stein; and the students in classrooms who revise, revise, revise.

Thanks to Adele Schroeter, Sarah Daunis, and the children of PS 59 for allowing me along with Scholastic staff into their school to shoot photographs for this book.

Thanks to my family: dearest Charles, sweet Cheryl, joyful Mark, and gentle Alex. Thanks for the dinners you cooked, the phone calls you fielded, and the computer glitches you fixed. And to Bailey, Ruby, Annie, Fifi, Sam, and Dixie... *now* it's time to play.

Thanks to Raymond Coutu, my patient editor at Scholastic. You taught me more about revision than anyone.

# FOREWORD

Revision should occur regularly in the writing workshop. However, for students to be successful at it, they need to have a sense of purpose and audience.

It's not unusual for preschoolers to write, even before using letters, because they have a purpose (such as creating a sign for their bedroom door to keep others out) and an audience (such as anyone who passes by the door). They select the appropriate size and type of paper and, typically, labor over the task until it is just right. They revise because their writing matters to them.

Contrast what preschoolers do naturally to what elementary students are usually assigned at the beginning of the school year: journal writing with the expectation to fill a page each day, in response to a question like "What would you like to write about?" Wouldn't it be more effective to give students more authentic assignments, based on questions like "What kind of writing will you do? What is your purpose and who is it for?" Questions like that get students thinking about and drafting pieces that embrace purpose and audience, which they can later revise if they so choose. In comparison, when students write without a sense of purpose and audience, there is little or no potential for revision. Fledgling writers come to believe that they have no audience besides their teacher, no purpose beyond completing the assignment, and, therefore, no real use for revision.

And it's all too easy for elementary students to get stuck in that way of thinking, particularly if they are coming from or going to classrooms where writing is not being exchanged regularly and read by peers, and there is little publishing going on. Meaningful assignments, high expectations, and clear routines need to be in place if we want students to revise.

So what a refreshing experience to read this book about teaching revision! Janet Angelillo provides no formulas, rules, labels, timetables, or plans that must be followed. Rather, she offers a wealth of extraordinarily helpful suggestions about teaching writing and about teaching revision as an important part of writing— specific suggestions such as using dialogue purposefully and broad suggestions such as understanding the difference between editing and revising. But this is not a book of isolated suggestions. Janet does not give us a list of teaching ideas to try, any more than she would give students a list of revision ideas to try. Instead, she demonstrates how to choose strategies shrewdly, based on what we learn about our students, and how to gradually fold those strategies into our daily routines. Each suggestion is embedded in a learning context, with a focus on modeling the types of revision strategies that solve particular problems and examples of how teachers and students have applied those strategies. The rubrics she includes are excellent assessment tools and useful guides for planning instruction.

Janet wisely says, "Children resist revising their writing because they can't see where writing needs work, and when they can see where it needs work, they don't know how to improve it. So it is essential that we explicitly teach students to recognize when they are not done, as well as concrete ways to revise their writing." As such, she provides all the tools we need to teach revision explicitly, using many real classroom examples. In her own teaching and by observing the teaching of others, she has seen students struggle with revision and has figured out ways to help them. Janet shares all this experience and knowledge, providing clear and manageable teaching suggestions, organized around a typical school year. In other words, she doesn't just tell us that students require explicit teaching about revision; she shows us how to do it.

There is a great deal of writing happening in school today, so students of all ages need more help with revision than ever. *Making Revision Matter* gives us the tools we need to provide that help. Students will learn to think about revision as an important part of writing, not just as one step in the writing process or as a way to please teachers. They come to see revision as a way to meet their purpose for writing and to speak to their audience. There is so much to learn from Janet Angelillo. She is an extremely talented teacher, coach, mentor, and writer, and we will be indebted to her for a long time for this logical, well-organized book—a book you will return to time and time again.

*by Diane Snowball*

# You Must Revise Your Life

A few years ago, my youngest child, Mark, left home for college. I watched in anguish as he moved everything to his dorm room, because my model of the perfect family did not include my "baby" living hundreds of miles away. To my distress, Mark was thrilled. He was ready to go and to grow. He was happy to be on his own at last.

But I wasn't. I had lived as "the mother" for so long that I knew little else beside selfless sacrifice—doing laundry, cooking meals, waiting up nights, shopping for "just the right" clothes, helping with homework, taxiing to social events, listening to unusual music. These things defined who I thought I was.

Then Mark went away.

And I no longer knew what to do.

My dear friend Phoebe took me under her wing. She became my mentor in finding happiness inside the "empty nest." She counseled and supported me; she showed me that it was time to revise my life. It was time to re-envision myself as a person, as a teacher, and as a mother. Time to imagine doing yoga, spinning yarn, rescuing animals, and becoming politically active. Sure, I knew these activities existed, but I was too busy smothering my kids to pursue them. Who was I if I was not their mother, if I was not doing things for them? The poet William Stafford teaches us that we must revise our lives, but I avoided revising until a wise mentor took my hand and guided me. I guess, in some ways, I just didn't know *how*.

In truth, I was living my life the way many students live their writing lives. I had a sense of duty. I did things for others, but I did not do things for myself. Often young writers write to please the teacher, because they've not yet learned that writing, like living, can be pleasing and fulfilling. In the same way that I had a narrow view of mothering, some students have a narrow view of writing, and they cannot, or will not, see possibilities for anything else. They cannot imagine a writing journey that directs them toward richness, toward change, toward a strong sense of self. This probably comes from negative perceptions about themselves. Young writers often do not identify themselves as writers, nor do they imagine writing as something they might do other than to fulfill school requirements or placate the teacher.

Too often, young children come to school drawing and scribbling and loving to write, but school shakes that passion out of them. Rather than teaching them to express their thoughts and to love words, and honoring their experiments with language, we offer them rules and assignments. Writing becomes a chore. Because it belongs to the teacher, it's too much effort, too much work. Children are all too often happy to hand in their work and be done with it, because, after all, once it's in the teacher's hands, it's the teacher's problem. Sometimes they have so little confidence in themselves as writers—so little respect for themselves or their audience—that they depend on teachers to "fix it all up." They haven't discovered that writing is pouring one's heart onto the page, and that revising is bigger and more important than recopying or checking spelling. They haven't learned that revision makes all the difference in the world, that knowing how to assess and apply findings not only strengthens one's work, but strengthens one's confidence as well. They do not yet know that the process of revision is discovery, and that discovery is power, and often fun.

If you've ever watched children play video games, you know they have the capacity for revision: They play games over and over until they've "beaten" their electronic foes, and they try trapdoors, weaponry, and lines of attack until they win. They talk with friends about how to succeed in the game, about the strategies they have tried, and they eagerly read guidebooks for suggestions about other strategies they can use. How can these be the same students who refuse to revise? How can they be the students who shrug and say they are happy with their first-draft writing? The answer is simple: video games matter to them. The challenge is making writing matter to them as much as games, making them see that revising their writing is as much about self-improvement as being the hero in a video game.

Revision means looking at fledgling efforts without guilt or self-chastisement. For writers, this can take the pressure off when writing a first draft. It means we can get it all "wrong" at first and it doesn't matter. We can always revise it and make it better. To do this, though, we must view writing and thinking as processes. William Stafford says that when he revises a poem it's not because the poem is bad,

*Similar to revision in many ways. Good analogy*

but because there must be more to it (1986). Too many students don't have that view. Instead, they focus on the product, on the finished piece of writing. They take little joy in seeing their minds at work while writing. Why? As mentioned earlier, maybe they're writing only to please the teacher or to complete an assignment. Or maybe writing is just too hard for them. They believe that if they can depend on the teacher to tell them how to fix it, they can relax a little. What they don't understand is that being able to do it *without* the teacher is what matters, just like playing baseball or riding a skateboard or playing the guitar. There is a time for being taught and coached, but then they must go off on their own. Furthermore, young writers don't yet understand that revision actually provides time to get to know themselves as writers. It can take the pressure off. It can be comforting.

Revision is power. It gives all of us ways to find out what we think and want to say, and ways to work toward clarity, passion, and meaning. It gives us ways to make our thinking visible and to negotiate with words, because thinking is seldom clear and perfect in its infantile form. It gives us the power to know how and when to change.

Most of all, revision is a way to live. We revise so many things in our lives—our hair, clothing, diets, relationships, interests, concerns, and careers. In fact, I would not want to live in a world where thoughts and opinions aren't being frequently revised, where life is stagnant and decidedly last-century. I want to live in a world in which politics are challenged, traditional beliefs are reconsidered, and technology and medicine move at light speed to make our lives better. I believe that teaching children to revise their writing is a model for teaching them to live: it teaches them to take a revisionist stance in everything they do, to expect and embrace change, and to position themselves to assess and solve problems in their world.

# WHAT THIS BOOK CONTAINS

In my work as a literacy consultant, I see firsthand how difficult teaching and learning revision can be. Too often teachers and students alike cringe at the thought. When I had my own classroom, my students sometimes devised elaborate schemes to make me believe they'd revised—changing colored pencils, cutting pages apart and retaping them, adding random words from a thesaurus. Of course, I realize now that my students felt lost and frustrated by revision because

Example
Bring in sketched "Help" Person across flow... Is that fun? No.
Why not ??
It's the same w/ revision.
You need to do it on your own.

of the ineffective way I taught it. In every grade I taught, from first to eighth, revision was a battle. As a staff developer for the Teachers College Reading and Writing Project, I saw again how students who easily and eagerly spilled ideas onto the page froze with resentment when asked to revise. In my current work, I continue to see students ignoring or resisting revision. This book is my effort to change all that. It demonstrates that specific, careful teaching empowers students to revise with confidence, clarity, and conviction.

Chapter 1 examines ways you can establish revision routines in writing workshop and change students' reluctance to acceptance by priming them for revision. Chapter 2 looks at assessing student needs and determining what revision work needs to be done at the start of the school year. This chapter offers numerous ways to improve writing dramatically and quickly. Chapter 3 looks at teaching students to read as writers do and to "apprentice" themselves to writers they love as a way to become better writers themselves. After all, studying "at the feet of a master" can change our writing profoundly. Joyce Carol Oates (2003) tells us that every writer has learned from others, and that the voice of Lewis Carroll is strong in her writing because he is the writer she read and studied as a child. Katie Ray (2002) tells us that what we "know by heart" will find its way into our writing. Chapters 4 and 5 look at studying mentor authors to revise fiction and nonfiction writing, and Chapter 6 considers qualities of good writing as a way to frame any revision course of study.

Chapter 7 surveys the whole school year by exploring the work we can do from September through June to support our students' ongoing growth as revisers. We must be sure to keep the big picture in mind as we teach revision, that ultimately students must know how to revise on their own, lest they end up with lists of strategies, or ways to revise, but no clue about when to use them. In Chapter 8 we'll look at a model for a unit of study in which students commit to advanced revision work in the spring after they've done a considerable amount of writing. This unit focuses on building independence as students look back on "old" writing, decide on revisions, and assess how they've grown as writers. Chapter 9 examines the ongoing issue of written conventions—grammar and punctuation—and how they can be used not only to correct writing but also to enhance it. Finally, in Chapter 10 we'll look at assessing student work and our own teaching, and using those results to plan a revision curriculum.

Our challenge is to teach students to value (and even love) revision and to come to know it, as Toni Morrison says, as "the most delicious part." Revision must become a habit of mind for writing and living. In fact, Donald Graves (1994) tells us that "the teacher who wishes the child to rethink his work wants above all for the child to begin to trust his own thinking and to see himself as someone who can solve problems on his own." Teaching revision is teaching students to *solve problems* on their own, and the result is sharper and more original thinking. Revising is not merely one step in a process nor is it done to please us. Without a higher purpose for revising, students often produce random and misdirected revisions that result in no improvement to the final product (Failgley & White, 1984).

When Mark left for college, my life required some deep revisions. Making them took courage, support, and hard work. Revising writing also takes courage, support, and hard work. Yet it is the revision process that teaches us so much about ourselves. I look at my revised self and I'm proud of what I see, although I see areas that still need work—the ongoing struggle to be smarter, more compassionate, more generous, and, yes, thinner, always thinner. Revision takes time, but it brings me closer to a vision of what life should be.

Revision spills over into my professional life, where I work beside elementary- and middle-school teachers in urban and suburban schools, on the east and west coasts, in the Midwest and in Canada. I think constantly about how I can revise my work; I study writing and teaching to become better at them.

Writing and living require revision. As we revise, we begin to see clearly and act deliberately, yet we surprise ourselves occasionally. With the help of mentors, we develop strategies for energizing writing, for combating boredom and frustration, and for being independent of others. We take pride in the revision we've done and discover new directions and possibilities. Ultimately, we must revise because, in writing and in life, it is the journey that counts.

# CHAPTER ONE

# GETTING INTO
# THE HABIT
# OF REVISION

I magine this. You are in an elementary classroom and it is time for writing. The teacher gives a lesson designed to get students started on an extended project, writing a personal narrative, and sends them off to get started. Some students stare at the page, some sharpen pencils, and others scribble diligently. The teacher confers with individual students about their writing and works with small groups. Apart from the teacher's soft voice and those of the students with whom he is talking, the room is quiet.

Then the inevitable happens: One child finishes writing, and the minute his pencil leaves the paper, he shouts, "I'm done!" One after another, the remaining students announce the same thing, as if the first writer has set the pace for a race.

They put their papers in the teacher's "completed work" box and never expect to work on them again. The teacher does what he can to cajole them into looking at those papers, but they shake their heads and say they are happy with the results. With the exception of some spelling and punctuation changes, and recopying, the writing stays the same. The teacher ends up grading papers that are close to the originals, only neater.

Unfortunately, this scenario is all too common. Getting students to revise their writing is frustrating and puzzling for so many teachers. In vain they implore students to go back and make their writing "better." They try to convince students that revision is essential. They teach revision strategies, such as "show, don't tell" or "use strong verbs," hoping that students will use them thoughtfully and with purpose. They talk about the importance of knowing how to improve writing, and of realizing that writing is a multilayered task that helps writers to grow understanding (Fulwiler, 2003). Still, their students remain reluctant to revise.

This phenomenon is epidemic. Teachers everywhere worry that students who won't revise won't be effective writers, and therefore certainly won't perform well on required writing tasks such as content area writing and state writing assessments. We all want to teach students how and when to revise and get them to do it, which is precisely the aim of this book.

In this chapter, I look at some reasons why students resist revision and ways we can help. I also examine ways to begin changing students' negative feelings about revision and show you how to "set them up" for daily, ongoing revision. This includes putting structures in place to ensure that students have the tools they need. I also offer specific lessons for establishing revision routines. I firmly believe that many children resist revising their writing because they can't see where their writing needs work, and when they can see where it needs work, they don't know how to improve it. So it is essential that we explicitly teach students to recognize when they are not finished and to provide concrete ways to revise their writing. We will look at the following topics:

- revision's place in the writing process

- the reasons students resist revision

- ways to help students embrace revision

# Revision's Place in the Writing Process

By now, the steps in the writing process are well known to most teachers. But I present them here to provide an overview of the best context in which to teach revision. While these steps are not set in stone and do not need to be followed in a linear way, they are a good starting point (Calkins, 1994; Graves, 1983). Writers eventually find their own ways of working. They invent a process that works for them (Fletcher, 2000), but I urge you to begin here. Revision is one step in the process and needs to be taught as such. Resist the temptation to focus too much on the earlier steps, leaving no energy for revision. Revision is where students do some of their best thinking.

**COLLECTING:** Writers collect their ideas. Many teachers ask students to keep a writer's notebook, where they practice leading a writer's life by recording possible ideas for later writing projects. Thus, my notebook observation of my dog's antics might later grow into a story or poem about my dog or an informational article on Labrador retrievers. Here are some suggestions for the types of writing that can go into a writer's notebook: memories, observations, responses to others' writing, complaints, overheard conversations, lists, parts of a draft, recollections sparked by reading or listening to literature, word collections, found poems, interesting or unusual facts, questions, character sketches, reactions to photos or pictures from magazines and newspaper articles, fortune cookie messages, lines from songs.

**CHOOSING AN IDEA:** At this stage, the writer chooses an idea from his or her notes or a notebook entry that can grow into a larger piece of writing.

**NURTURING AND PLANNING:** The writer then collects information about the idea. This step is important because writers seldom write without planning, although occasionally they plan informally by talking with others or just thinking about their writing. For students, planning may include freewriting to discover more about their idea, doing research, interviewing others, thinking about it from different angles, zooming in to sketch one small portion of the idea, deciding what's important about it, jotting down phrases to include in a draft, planning by using a graphic organizer, and choosing a genre to write in.

**DRAFTING:** The writer begins composing, creating what Donald Murray (1985) calls "the discovery draft" because it is an experiment for getting to the heart of what he wants to write. By drafting, the writer discovers what he knows, what he needs to know, whether he has a subject worth addressing, if he needs to limit the subject, if the genre works, if the structure works, and if there is voice (Murray, 1985). Drafting is generally not done in the notebook but on loose sheets of paper that can be clipped to the back of the final piece to show the stages of thought.

**REVISING:** The writer works to make the writing match his intention, often returning to the note-book as a way to try out possibilities. Often a writer returns to the collecting part of his process to flesh out more ideas or to find words, phrases, or whole passages. He may also study one or more published texts to find techniques for revision. He may explore structure, purpose, audience, genre, word choice, written conventions to convey meaning—the possibilities are endless. The writer uses all his writing tools to make his writing clear.

**PROOFREADING:** The writer checks over spelling, grammar, and punctuation for accuracy.

**PUBLISHING:** The writer sends the writing into the world, ideally in celebration with other writers and with the expectation of getting responses from readers.

## The Teacher as Writer in the Writing Workshop

We learn so much about teaching writing by tackling the writing process ourselves. This activity gives our teaching authority and honesty, and it allows us to figure out the content of our teaching by working through difficulties we encounter. Many writing teachers (Calkins, 1994; Graves, 1994; Murray, 1985) encourage us to do this. Tom Romano (1987) tells us that children learn best from teachers who "actually get in the water with them." Regie Routman (1996) urges us to let our students see us go through the same struggles they do. When we write, our lessons are sharper, our teaching smarter. Save your revisions during the school year and make note of your questions, your intentions, your general feelings. This will not only make you a better writer and teacher of writing, but it will give you rich material to use in mini-lessons and conferences. Put these onto overhead transparencies and you will have authentic samples of many revision strategies, as well as notes about how each one worked for you.

## Bottom-Line Teaching Practices in the Writing Workshop

For effective teaching and learning, the following activities should happen every day:

**PRESENTING A MINI-LESSON:** This is a short, precise, direct teaching lesson in which the teacher teaches a writing skill through demonstration or modeling. The content of the lesson can be about genre, routines, or any part of the writing process, such as adding dialogue or refining transitions. We teach students how to revise through this type of direct teaching.

**WRITING AND CONFERRING:** This is an extended block of time when the students are composing and crafting, and the teacher is conferring with individuals or small groups. Frequently, conferring focuses on revision strategies tailored to individual student needs.

**SHARING:** During the last five minutes of workshop, the teacher asks one or two students to share their thinking—that is, to talk about their writing process and how it went that day. Often students with whom the teacher has conferred are among the first to share. This is not a time for writers to showcase their writing, but rather a time to share thoughts about how strategies for writing have or have not worked in practical situations.

## Units of Study in the Writing Workshop

Mary Ellyn Lehner teaches sixth grade in Bethel, Connecticut. Her goal for writing workshop this year is to build her class's revision knowledge. She begins the year with a quick assessment, such as the one described in Chapter 2, and moves into teaching three to five new strategies per "unit of study," in addition to teaching revision in small groups and conferences. Typically, the annual writing workshop schedule is organized into units of study (Nia, 1999). A unit of study ranges from

FIGURE 1-1

## Suggested Timeline for a Unit of Study

**WEEK ONE:** Collect ideas, become immersed in the genre, talk with others about the genre

**WEEK TWO:** Choose topic, plan and research, write first draft

**WEEK THREE:** Revise—teach one new strategy per day

**WEEK FOUR:** Edit and proofread, prepare draft for publication, celebrate, reflect

two to six weeks, during which the class studies one topic in great depth (Calkins et al., 2003). Topics can be genre-based, such as writing personal narratives, essays, or poetry, and craft-based, such as revision. A good curriculum calendar includes both. Think of units of study as the bones upon which we build instruction. When planning units of study, consider the entire school year and be sure to include variety and depth, as well as state or district requirements.

An individual unit of study generally consists of immersion and investigation, followed by planning for writing, drafting, and revising. (See Figure 1-1 for a sample timeline.) The units end with celebration, reflection, and accommodation for weaving lessons learned into ongoing writing work. See Appendix F for one school's writing curriculum plan.

In order to create structures to support revision, Mary Ellyn establishes a "revision corner," where she displays her ongoing charts of revision strategies, examples from books where writers have used the technique she's taught, and stages of student writing that show the strategies in action. Mary Ellyn encourages her students to "research" ways to revise by reading pages she's flagged in books about revision, by meeting with revision partners in the writing corner, by adding examples from their own writing to the charts, and by developing ongoing revision questions for which they will all search for answers. (See Figure 1-2.) In addition, Mary Ellyn's writing rubric, which she uses to hold students accountable, contains a section on revision. (See Appendix E.)

Looking at and planning extended revision study can go a long way toward making our teaching and our students' writing stronger. Shifting our attention to revision and modeling how much we value it shows students that revision is a

FIGURE 1-2

## Students' Ongoing Revision Questions

- How do we make something that's interesting to us become interesting to our readers?

- How do we get a message into the story without just telling what it is?

- How can we make the middles of writing as interesting as the beginnings?

- How can we keep endings from just fizzling out?

- How do we find exciting words to use without just using the dictionary all the time?

- How can we get voice into our writing?

- How can we write better plans so our revising is easier?

- How can we figure out what to revise when it looks good to us?

- How can we spell and punctuate better so rereading our writing is easier?

major part of what we do in writing workshop, and that it is here to stay. We must teach students to position themselves to be revisers for life.

## HOW YOU MIGHT COVER REVISION IN ANY UNIT OF STUDY

Setting aside five to eight days for revision instruction gives students the implicit message that revision is important. But what should we teach during those days? Here are some lesson ideas:

- rereading at regular intervals, including at the end of a sentence, paragraph or page, and for five minutes at the end of a writing session

- reading work aloud softly to hear how it sounds

- asking a partner to read your work to hear how a reader would read it; peer conferring about revision; discussing honestly the merits and pitfalls of revision

- marking a draft at places that need revision

- using ideas about writing from a mentor author to make plans for revision (see Chapter 3 for ideas on how to use authors' work)

- making revisions according to genre and qualities of good writing (see Chapter 6)

- making decisions to use revision strategies you've already practiced in another piece; using the class revision chart to get ideas for revision

- using tools such as colored pencils and sticky notes to support revision

# THE REASONS STUDENTS RESIST REVISION

Students resist revising for a number of reasons, including misunderstanding for whom they are writing, confusing revising and editing, and focusing more on product than on process. The next few sections will help you see revision from the students' perspective and understand why we must teach revision explicitly.

## Students View the Teacher as Their Sole Audience

Many students see writing as a requirement to satisfy their teachers, and teachers as their one and only audience. If they write only to fulfill an assignment, there is little reason for revision, because there is often little investment in the writing from the beginning. Furthermore, since writing belongs to the teacher and not to them, children are often satisfied with surface-level changes, such as "cleaning up" punctuation and changing words occasionally. They don't take time for organizing and expanding information, creating transitions, deleting and subordinating information, and improving syntactic structures (Boiarsky, 1981).

Lisa Schofield is an experienced workshop teacher who teaches fourth grade in Irvington, New York. However, through conferring, she discovered that her students consider revision something they are required to do *for her*, not something that helps them as writers (Calkins, 1983). Their attitude shows her that perhaps it is time to reexamine the way she teaches revision. She knows that, by fourth grade, students should view revision more purposely and thoughtfully (Calkins, 1983).

Based on her observations, Lisa decides that revision work should focus on developing a sense of audience, speaking clearly through writing to people her students know, such as schoolmates, family members, cafeteria workers, and the visitors at the senior center. Lisa designs revision work early in the year that emphasizes knowing one's audience and writing to that audience.

In writing workshop classrooms, students come to realize that one purpose of writing is to communicate one's thinking to others—many others, not just the teacher. However, students often fail to understand that the process of revision will make their thinking clearer, stronger, and more meaningful to them and their readers. Knowing that the students in Mr. Smith's class down the hall will read their stories may make students more eager to revise.

## Students Don't Receive Explicit Teaching in Revision

Another reason students resist revision may be a lack of specific teaching about revision. By and large, students don't know precisely what good writers do when they revise, yet we know they benefit from direct instruction in revision strategies (Fitzgerald & Markham, 1987). Many teachers talk about the importance of features such as exciting beginnings and varied sentences, but they provide little direct teaching on exactly what writers do to create these features. So even the well-meaning student gets discouraged, much as I would if a baseball coach ordered me to hit a home run without any direct instruction on exactly how to do it—and, not to mention, *a lot* of practice on my own! At least if I knew how good ballplayers do it, I could give it a try, even if I was not successful at first. Without direct instruction, I'd give up before I even got going. So we must reconsider the explicitness of our teaching of revision.

## Students Confuse Revising With Editing

Sometimes students don't revise because their only experience with revision has been to recopy their teacher's "corrections" on their papers; they equate revision with editing (Chrenka, Balkema, Kuzma, & Vasicek, 1996). As a result, they find revision boring. When I don't know a lot about something, I often think it's boring. Not knowing the depth, nuances, and subtleties of, for example, symphony music, tennis, or computer games can make them appear boring. Some students have not had the experience of getting so good at something they become "experts." Encouraging students to engage in a deep study teaches them as much about *how to study* as about what topic they're studying. Thorough study of revision gives students the chance to experience revision to change and clarify meaning, and they will begin to see that it does much more than "clean up" their work.

## Students Focus Too Much on Product and Not Enough on Process

If we don't teach revision as a problem-solving skill, we miss the chance to teach students a critical-thinking skill. So we must examine not only what we are teaching but the purpose and spirit in which we are teaching it. Do we allow our concern for neatness to misdirect attention toward product rather than process? Do we minimize the importance of revision by presenting it as a chore—as a way of cleaning up sloppy writing? Do we steal revision's power by telling students what to revise in their writing, thus cheating them of important decision-making and problem-solving opportunities? Do we expect students to figure out on their own what to do with a piece of writing? Perhaps they pick up subtle signs from us that revision is tedious. Donald Murray (1995) says, "the teacher must model an attitude that emphasizes discovery and communication ... The teacher who knows firsthand the excitement of revision, and may even share examples of personal revision, may make an interest in revision contagious."

So perhaps students haven't received clear, direct instruction or seen the powerful results revision can produce. Perhaps they don't know that even their favorite writers work hard to "get it right." Teaching students to revise begins with getting students into a mind-set—that is, getting students to expect to revise at every stage of the writing process. In some ways, we can't blame students for not wanting to revise; we, as teachers, may have focused on product and de-emphasized revision's importance so much that they are only following our lead. In his book *Live Writing* (1999), Ralph Fletcher explains that teaching students specific strategies for revising is like giving them the tools they need to get the revision work done.

# Ways to Help Students Embrace Revision

Our attitudes and careful instruction in revision set the stage for revision. Before we teach students strategies, we must create a learning environment that will support revising. Students should come to expect that they will revise frequently. Donald Murray says that revising should be repeated as many times as necessary in order to produce a draft "worthy of editing" (1985), and the environment in the room should help students to view revision this way. This section defines components needed to establish this environment.

## Create an Expectation That Revision Will Occur Routinely in Writing Workshop

One summer day I met with a group of teachers from California in the school cafeteria. We made plans for the upcoming year, focusing on writing workshop and revision's place in it. As we listed revision strategies, one teacher threw up his hands, saying, "You don't know my kids, my sixth graders. They've never revised in their lives. They don't want to revise. In fact, they refuse to revise. If I ask them to revise, they shrug and say they like it the way it is. What do you do with kids like that?" He shook his head in frustration, as if to say, "It's hopeless." Other teachers in the room nodded.

What do we do with kids who refuse to revise? How do we get them to change? Obviously, teaching children from a very young age that they need to revise most of what they write is the best way to avoid this problem. However, older students may come to your class with a belief that revision doesn't matter or, at best, a belief that revision means recopying work neatly. In these cases, it becomes a matter of unteaching these beliefs and reteaching new ones, which takes time and patience. It requires developing a "philosophy of revision," a stance that we take, as writers and writing teachers, defining revision as important mind work.

As I talked with the California teachers, we recognized this as an almost universal problem. We determined that students' refusal to revise can often be traced to having little investment in their writing, a lack of knowledge about revision or faith in the value of it, and a sketchy sense of audience. We also realized that we may not be giving students adequate time to revise. Many of the teachers admitted to allowing very little space between their first and final drafts, which gives students the impression that revision is not important.

We can gradually build faith in what revision can do. Start with simple strategies, so students can see quick, meaningful results. (See page 42 for suggestions for simple revision strategies.) For example, the California teachers decided to focus on what students' favorite writers say about revision. They felt it was helpful for students to know that these writers work to get it right, and that writing is only partly inspiration and talent.

The teachers also decided to post a writing workshop timeline that clearly sets aside several days for revision. (See Figure 1-1.) They agreed that showing revision scheduled over several days would give students the clear message that revising is a major and essential part of the writing process. In the end, the implicit message is that revision is what writers do, with few or no exceptions.

## Model Good Attitudes Toward Revision

When we consider student attitudes toward revision, we might also think about the hidden messages we communicate to them. Katie Ray (2002) tells us curriculum grows out of thinking metacognitively about our own writing—the content of writing workshop. But her idea has implications about the silent messages we convey to students as well. How do we feel about revision? How do we revise our work? Do we consider revision an odious task? Do we ever actually revise our own writing? If we believe deep down that revision is boring or futile, then we will communicate that to our students. We will send out subtle signals that say, "This is the torturous part. Do it because, like taking medicine, it's good for you. But expect to hate it, because it's awful." We will inadvertently teach them that revision is the worst part of writing, rather than the most exciting.

We need to watch ourselves as we revise and examine our own beliefs, because we need to have a good attitude toward revision (or at least deliver Oscar-level performances to give that impression). Then we need to communicate to students that revising is not a choice. We don't give students a choice about whether to do math or science, nor would we ignore their refusals to show their work. Why do we accept this in writing? After all, revising is what writers do. They are in a revising state of mind, or should be, unless they're working on notebook entries or early drafts. Georgia Heard (2003) advises us to be honest with students about revision and to ask them how they feel about it. Honoring their feelings, while assuring them that we are going to help them feel more confident, will help students a great deal.

## Research on Revision Processes

Alice S. Horning is a researcher who has investigated writers' processes for revision. She believes that writers make revisions in their minds before, during, and after producing a text, in addition to the written revisions they produce (2002). She suggests that expert writers know a great deal about their own revision behaviors and make use of a wide range of skills to make their writing readable for others (2004). These skills are:

- metarhetorical awareness (knowing how to work at writing and the approaches that work)

- metastrategic awareness (knowing when to switch to other revision strategies because the current one isn't working)

- metalinguistic awareness (knowledge of language and the ability to evaluate the sound of one's text)

As we plan revision instruction, we can keep create opportunities for students to experience each skill area.

# Foster Student Ownership of Writing

We must help students understand that their writing belongs to them and that it reflects their thinking and mirrors what they want to say. Perhaps their voices have been silenced in some way; we can never truly know the circumstances from which some children come, nor the ways they have been taught to think about themselves and their writing. So we must give them the tools for thinking about their histories and using that information to inform who they are as writers. In fact, Donald Graves (1994) says, "When children become aware of how they have composed and solved problems in the past, they are more able to approach new problems in the future." We can teach students to hear their own voices and speak through their writing; then we must teach them how to express themselves clearly and precisely. This will happen much more quickly in a classroom where revision occurs routinely.

Often students legitimately don't know how to improve their writing. A quick assessment at the beginning of the year can help us determine how much students know. (See Chapter 2 for more on early assessments.) As we teach revision strategies at the beginning of the year, we should begin to see students using them and hold them accountable. One way is to ask students to highlight revisions in colored pencil, with a margin note explaining why they chose a particular strategy.

As I mentioned earlier, it's a good idea to use your own writing to model revision at the beginning of the year, but as time goes on, you may ask students for permission to photocopy and use their work in demonstrations. Also ask them to explain why and how each strategy worked so that you can use that information. Here are some questions to ask students about their revisions: What were you thinking as you did this revision? What was your intent as a writer? Why did you choose this revision strategy instead of another? Did you do anything else first that didn't work? What made you keep going until it worked? Asking students to think about these questions helps them to focus on their thinking and revision processes as ways to understand that they write for themselves, not just for the teacher.

## Encourage Students to Reread and Rethink Writing on a Daily Basis

Most students have not been taught, either implicitly or explicitly, to revisit or rethink their work. Yet if we watch them carefully, we notice that even young children instinctively know how to do this: They change the rules for games they have invented, or move walls of block houses they are building, or reshape the clay figures they have made. Older children do this, too. For example, when they play computer games, they go back to try other routes or attack strategies to "beat" the game. They "mess around" with songs and instruments, with bikes and skates, with balls and bats, trying to invent new ways to play. But when it comes to writing, they don't do this.

To help them, we must teach them that whatever they write is not carved in stone and that they can indeed "play with it" to get it the way they want it. To do this, they must be willing to step back and look at their writing many times, just as they do with sand castles. So we must build rereading into writing time, and demonstrate by rereading our own writing so students can see how we think. Writers who reread their writing come to understand better what they want to say. Allen Ramsey (1981) tells us that revising is not the linear activity many students believe it is, but rather a form of invention in which the writer discovers new ideas about what he wants to say.

We can build rereading into writing workshop by stopping students five minutes before the end of the allotted time and saying, "Writers, would you please take until the end of workshop to reread what you wrote today?" This will go a

FIGURE 1-3

## What to Do in the Five-Minute Reread

When students reread their writing in the few remaining minutes of workshop, they should notice if:

- they strayed from their topic

- the writing makes sense

- the punctuation helps them say what they mean

- they left something out (including chunks, phrases, punctuation, words)

- the writing is too messy to read back to themselves

- they want to add more

- they've stayed true to genre or if they need to change genre

They can assign themselves one revision to work on next time, marking it with a colored pencil; highlight a revision they made and jot down the thinking behind it; or read their writing aloud quietly to see how it sounds. Is it smooth?

## Drafting Techniques

I ask students to draft by rereading their plans in their notebooks, thinking about what they are going to write, closing their notebooks, and then drafting. Wendy Bishop (2004) calls this a "memory draft," because students often feel they must have forgotten something and need to revise after completing it. Bishop also suggests setting students up for revision by teaching them to draft in these ways:

**Draft recklessly:** students learn to trust that they have more ideas and become flexible about revision

**Draft generously:** students learn to ignore internal critics; they learn that invested writers tinker incessantly

**Draft out of order:** students learn to take advantage of the inventive, cyclical, recursive nature of composing; they learn to tolerate ambiguity and avoid premature closure

If we plan methods of drafting, we set the stage for revision to follow naturally.

long way toward getting them into the habit of rereading their writing. Students may not know exactly what to do while rereading for five minutes, so some mini-lessons may be needed. (See Figure 1-3 for ideas.) Ask students to note their thinking in the margins as they reread, and share those notes at the end of the workshop. Encourage them to use that information to plan more writing. Starting each subsequent writing session with five minutes of rereading and revision helps young writers to concentrate and "prime the writing pump."

Later on, show students that writers stop to reread as they revise. They reread paragraphs to see how they hold together, and they look back over words to see if they can make better choices. Eventually, writing becomes more fluid, clearly conveying the writer's thoughts.

Frequent rereading can save students from getting too far into a piece before making necessary changes. It can help students clarify thinking and head confidently in the right direction. And it can help them choose an appropriate genre— their personal essay may work better as a poem or a feature article. Rereading and rethinking in ways like these must happen daily in order for students to become comfortable and skilled in revision techniques.

# Helpful Professional Books

## On Writing Workshop

- *How's It Going? A Practical Guide to Conferring with Student Writers* by Carl Anderson (Heinemann, 2000)
- *The Art of Teaching Writing* by Lucy McCormick Calkins (Heinemann, 1994)
- *The No-Nonsense Guide to Teaching Writing* by Judy Davis and Sharon Hill (Heinemann, 2003)
- *Writing Workshop: The Essential Guide* by Ralph Fletcher and JoAnn Portalupi (Heinemann, 2001)
- *The Writing Workshop: Getting Through the Hard Parts (and They're All Hard Parts)* by Katie Wood Ray (NCTE, 2001)

I encourage you to read these books if you're interested in learning more about the structures and details of writing workshop and the writing process. Perhaps your colleagues will be willing to meet informally to discuss one or more of these books in light of your own teaching. (See Appendix C for suggestions on forming study groups.)

## On Revision

- *The Revision Toolbox: Teaching Techniques That Work* by Georgia Heard (Heinemann, 2003) is a wonderful book about creating an atmosphere in the class that supports revision. Heard presents many revision lessons and suggestions for creating revision centers.
- *After THE END: Teaching and Learning Creative Revision* by Barry Lane (Heinemann, 1993) is filled with ideas for teaching revision. His strategies such as "explode the moment" and "snapshots and thought-shots" have helped children everywhere to revise.

## With Sections on Revision

- *6 + 1 Traits of Writing: The Complete Guide, Grades 3 and Up* by Ruth Culham (Scholastic, 2003)
- *Teaching Elaboration and Word Choice* by Leann Nickelsen (Scholastic, 2001)
- *Revising & Editing: Using Models and Checklists to Promote Successful Writing Experiences* by Les Parsons (Pembroke, 2001)
- *Brighten Up Boring Beginnings and Other Quick Writing Lessons (Grades 4 and Up)* by Laura Robb (Scholastic, 2003)
- *Teaching Powerful Writing: 25 Short Read-Aloud Stories with Lessons That Motivate Students to Use Literary Elements in Their Writing* by Bob Sizoo (Scholastic, 2001)
- *Helping Students Revise Their Writing: Practical Strategies, Models, and Mini-Lessons That Motivate Students to Become Better Writers* by Marianne Tully (Scholastic, 1996)

## Children's Literature in Writing Workshop

Picture books, chapter books, poetry, nonfiction books that you love, and literature that you know well and have read many times are important teaching tools. I draw on these books when I need inspiration to revise and answers to my revision questions. I may study how Sharon Creech created a character's voice in *Walk Two Moons* or how Toni Morrison handled the passage of time in *The Bluest Eye*. The books you love can teach you and your students how to write and revise. Studying them can help you and your students figure out what to change in your writing and theirs (Ray, 1999; Harwayne, 1992). It can lift writing from mere proficiency to art. Great writing teachers have pointed us this way for decades, and it is a skill that will have immeasurable worth for student writers.

# Build in Time for Partner and Small-Group Work

The children's writer Mem Fox (1992) says, "If I didn't talk about my writing, how would I know what to improve? In fact, rewriting is often synonymous with retalking to anyone who'll listen."

If we want students to improve their writing, we must provide them with opportunities to talk about it with others. Beverly Falk (2000) tells us, "Social interaction is critical to learning. We need to talk, question, and comment with others about what we are coming to know." This process of "coming to know," or working toward understanding, is essential for high-order thinking and problem solving. Hearing our words read aloud, as well as explaining what we meant, helps enrich and extend our understanding. Of course, some teachers point out that inexperienced writers occasionally give the "wrong" advice to each other about revision. Alas, this is the downside of partner work, but it is still worth the risk, because talking with others is valuable for constructing learning (Bruner, 1986; Duckworth, 1996; Vygotsky, 1986).

I've found that it is most helpful for students to have a writing partner and to remain with that partner for a few weeks or even months to build trust and understanding. Reading one's writing aloud to a partner is powerful, especially when we teach students to ask their partners to listen for use of particular strategies, such as whether the dialogue sounds realistic.

Sean is a fifth grader in a public school in New York City. He enjoys writing but lacks confidence. He makes few revisions to his writing because he feels there is nothing he can do to improve it. So Sean's teacher pairs him with two other writers who seem to each have different writing strengths, ranging from writing good beginnings to organizing. The teacher has them meet twice a week for revision. Each student brings a section of a draft, along with a targeted question for the others in the group. Their questions are based on rereading their writing to ascertain where they might need help and referencing a classroom chart of revision strategies the teacher has already taught.

On the day I visit, Sean is reading the beginning of his story to his partners. His question for them is, "Do you like my story?"

I explain that questions like that may not be targeted enough to be helpful, and that, frankly, it doesn't matter whether your partners like your story or not.

What matters is getting feedback from partners on the writing itself, and that questions such as "How can I make my lead more interesting?" and "Can you picture what my cousin looks like in this story?" promote feedback.

Sean changes his question to "Are there any words that are used too much?," which gives his partners a focus for the revision meeting. His partners can help Sean think about ways to improve one section of his writing.

Partners can help each other in every step of the process. The simple act of reading one's writing aloud to a partner helps enormously. It teaches students to listen carefully to one another and to respond thoughtfully. Further, hearing one's own voice reading aloud can make a writer discover places where writing can be revised.

## Making the Most of Partner Work

Once you've set up partnerships for revising, be sure to teach students exactly what they should say and do. You can teach them to help each other by

- encouraging them to avoid revising everything at once. Rather, have them focus on one aspect of the writing, such as word choice, the beginning, or how strong the ending is.

- thinking back on a mini-lesson to decide what to listen or read for.

- looking at the classroom revision chart, which records all the strategies the teacher has taught so far, and choose something to read for.

- reading their partners' writing twice before making any decisions.

- thinking about a mentor author that might help a partner.

- not telling their partner exactly what words to change, because that would prevent him or her from doing the revising independently.

- asking their partner if the advice makes sense to him or her.

- talking about revisions after they have been made to evaluate whether they worked.

- adding their name to their partner's work so their revision suggestions will be recognized.

- putting their suggestions in writing to clarify them and so their partner won't forget what they are.

## Dealing with Spelling

Writers must be able to spell or, at least, be able to proofread their spelling. The primary purpose of spelling is to enable readers to read a text. Diane Snowball and Faye Bolton (1999) tell us that "competent spellers use many strategies in tackling unfamiliar words, and growth in the range of these strategies should be part of children's writing strengths and need."

Direct instruction in spelling strategies is essential, as is providing opportunities for shared, interactive, guided, and independent writing practice. Students must understand strategies for spelling rather than relying on someone to spell words for them or becoming too dependent on a word wall. Exercising their spelling muscles by learning and applying strategies builds independence.

Students may want to check their spelling and grammar on the computer. While this is useful, it is equally important for them to learn to read over their work slowly and carefully. While computers perform amazing functions, ultimately students are responsible for their writing. There are times when spell- and grammar-checks are not options for them, such as on most state tests and job applications, so students must be able to write without them. Teaching students to rely mainly on themselves helps them become independent writers. For more help in teaching spelling, see *Spelling in Use* by Lester Laminack and Katie Wood Ray (NCTE, 1996), and *Spelling K–8* by Diane Snowball and Faye Bolton (Stenhouse, 1999).

## Teach the Difference Between Revision and Proofreading

When I went to school, admittedly a long time ago, my classmates and I were not taught to revise. "Revision" meant going back and "checking your spelling and punctuation" and then "making a clean copy" to hand in. There was no talk of significant ways to improve the work; it was merely an exercise to produce something neat for the bulletin board. While I do believe that student work should be readable and mechanically accurate, having them check over spelling, grammar, and punctuation is proofreading, not revising, although writers can use these conventions as ways to shape meaning (Angelillo, 2002; Ray, 1999). Punctuation, spelling, and grammar become craft tools that writers apply as they revise. I look at this in more detail in Chapter 9.

Revising means making serious changes to get closer to what the writer needs and wants to say. Proofreading means checking over the nearly completed writing to be sure it is accurate according to acceptable standards. Both steps are necessary and both help clarify meaning so readers can access the writer's message. But proofreading comes when the writing is nearly done, whereas revision is ongoing and, ideally, begins earlier in the process. Proofreading involves minor changes and "cleanup," while revising often involves changing major parts of a piece. Donald Murray (1995) says that revisers think ahead toward the next draft, while editing and proofreading are angled toward preparing for the reader and the final draft. Ralph Fletcher and JoAnn Portalupi (2001) tell us to "construct a brick wall" between revising and editing or proofreading: "Revision is a composing tool; editing involves the surface features of the writing."

If we devote a significant block of time during a writing unit to revision, students will get the message that "checking it over" is not what we mean. Surely we would not expect them to "check something over" for a week! By demonstrating revision of our own work, we show that we mean major changes. Finally, by naming proofreading as such, and giving students only a short time before the publication date to do it (except, of course, for students with motor difficulties or those who struggle with conventions and recopying), we clarify what we mean and remove any misconceptions about the differences between revision and proofreading.

## Celebrate Accomplishments

When students complete writing, be sure to celebrate their accomplishments by having them share their writing with others in the school. This not only creates community but also helps students understand that writers write for real audiences. It can also make them work harder on their writing because they know they'll be sharing it with others. Ralph Peterson (1992) says, "When we celebrate in the learning community, we recognize that people have the power to incorporate the joys and achievements of other people into their lives. Celebration not only dignifies the lives of individuals and the group, it contributes to a sense of belonging."

Celebrations do not have to be large affairs. Something as simple as having one table of students read their writing to another table can do the job. Students don't need to read entire pieces either, but can share a favorite line or paragraph or talk about the place where they did their best revision. This encourages even the most reluctant writer to share. You might also build in spontaneous, daily celebrations. For example, you could recognize immediately when a reluctant writer tries a revision strategy. You could post student writing in common areas and attach comment sheets.

That said, big celebrations can be fun. You may want to schedule parent nights, grade-wide readings, or small "open-mike" after-school meetings to build community-wide support for your students' writing and revision work.

# SUMMARY

When we teach students routines for revision, it becomes a part of their writing lives. Students often want to rush off to the next "activity" if we do not slow them down by requiring them to reread and discuss their work. Before we can dig deeply into revision, we must establish healthy writing rituals in the room, such as meeting regularly to discuss writing, being respectful of each other's work, and celebrating finished work. We can also model in actions and words that revision is something we do in all parts of our lives. Building in time for revision and giving students the tools they need to do it well sets the stage for meaningful and ongoing revision throughout the year.

## Some Points to Remember

- Teach students to reread their writing frequently.

- Set aside a few minutes at the end of each writing session for rereading.

- Teach students to take notes for revising as they reread.

- Keep supplies available for revision (small pieces of paper, colored pencils, highlighters, glue, sticky notes) and teach students how to use them.

- Devote significant time to revision instruction in each unit of study that you plan.

- Make revising a life skill that resurfaces throughout the day, such as in art (revising a painting), at lunch (revising seating arrangements), or in science (revising an experiment).

# CHAPTER TWO

# INTRODUCING REVISION EARLY IN THE SCHOOL YEAR

**F**all beckons us back to classrooms and to the excitement that every new school year brings. Dawn arrives later, and dusk creeps in earlier. The morning air is sharp and cool, and evening air is filled with the smell of fireplace smoke. Students come with new clothes, pencils, and notebooks; they are filled with expectation and, sometimes, trepidation. In a way, they come to us having revised themselves. They've played long and hard all summer. They've grown taller, lost teeth and grown new ones, and seem somehow different. Many come ready to experience whatever we have in store for them. They know that a new school year requires changing from an old self to a new one. They are ready and waiting for new and exciting ways to learn. Therefore, at the very beginning of the school year, we can assess their work and plan a year of revision in writing workshop.

In this chapter I look at revision work teachers can do early in the school year. Specifically, I examine the part assessment plays in this early work. While one goal in writing workshop is to teach students to draft, another is to teach them to revise. Consequently, we need to assess at the beginning of the year what they already know about revision. To that end, we'll look at one teacher's early-year assessment work. From there, I'll show you how to

- assess students to determine revision strategies for a first unit of study

- use assessment results to plan the unit of study

- carry out the unit of study

## ONE TEACHER'S EARLY-YEAR ASSESSMENT WORK

I visit Connie Wu's fifth-grade class one morning in early September. Connie has her students gathered together in the meeting area. She explains that, over the next three days, she needs to get to know them as writers so she can address their needs in writer's workshop.

"I want to know each of you well, because each of you is different," she says. "I'm going to ask you to write something for me today in writing workshop. I'm not going to tell you what to write, because that would be taking choices away from you. Choice is important because it teaches you to be independent and to have confidence in your ability to think and to write. So you can write whatever you want. I'm going to give you time today to write a draft, and time tomorrow to revise it. By the next day, we'll finish up and you can hand them in."

Connie sends the students off to write. Once they're settled in, she observes them and take notes. "I can learn so much from just watching them for a while," she whispers to me. "I also want to confer with some of them, but right now I'm learning what they know about writing by just watching them."

This is true. We immediately see students who have strategies for getting themselves to write, students who write slowly, and students who seem unacquainted with paper and pen. Connie goes around to talk to them individually, coaching those who have very little on their paper. She takes careful notes about these students because their actions might be either indicators of difficulty or merely back-to-school anxiety.

Connie also notes children who write easily. Is their ability the result of writing over the summer? Understanding strategies for getting their writing going quickly? A combination of both? And, despite their ability to generate writing, is the work original and lively, or trite and lifeless? This initial writing assessment teaches Connie so much about her new class. She observes their writing processes and reads their writing each of the three nights. She plans her instruction based on results from a rubric she uses. (See Figure 2-1 for a rubric that you can use at the start of the year.) While Connie understands that students can be at different places depending on what they are writing and the time of the year, the rubric provides a quick way for her to assess what they know now. She will work with students throughout the year, individually and in small groups, to help them become independent revisers. (See Figure 2-2 for ways she may accomplish this.)

The next day, Connie asks her students to revise their drafts using any method they know. Observing what they do and do not know will help her plan a course of action. Her intention is to assess the class's range of knowledge about revision, not just to help strugglers. She confers with some students, carefully choosing among a cross section of those who appear lost and those who are work-ing hard. She asks them to tell her how they are revising their writing.
Here are some of the things they say:

> "I know that I put in some dialogue."

> "I can add more to the end."

> "I could make the beginning better."

> "I like it the way it is. Do I have it make it longer?"

> "I don't like to write."

> "What do you want me to do?"

> "I guess I can change a few words if you want."

Immediately Connie sees that most of their knowledge about revision is too broad. For example, "I know I put in some dialogue" only makes sense in certain genres of writing and for certain purposes. In the case above, Sarah is writing a

# A Rubric for Assessing Revision
# Early in the School Year

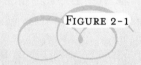

FIGURE 2-1

**STAGE-ONE REVISER**

- looks piece over without purpose

- does little or no proofreading

- hands in piece without much thought

- recopies to make it neater

- inserts obvious words that were left out

- resists revision completely

**STAGE-TWO REVISER**

- adds a few words (often at end of piece) to make it a little longer

- changes one or two words

- rereads by skimming and makes only a few changes

- uses mentor texts sparingly

- tries some revision strategies, such as adding dialogue or changing the beginning, but without purpose

**STAGE-THREE REVISER**

- adds and removes words strategically

- begins to revise with meaning and audience in mind

- knows some revision strategies and uses them deliberately

- uses punctuation deliberately, accurately, and as a revision tool

- changes beginnings and endings thoughtfully

- is able to articulate the writing's purpose

- pays attention to word choice

- recognizes the value of revision and expects to revise

- adds strategies to revision repertoire

- is comfortable using mentor text

- asks for specific help in writing conferences

**STAGE-FOUR REVISER**

- is able to change sequence and reorganize chunks of writing

- is able to make deeper revisions, including changing genre

- has ability to look critically at his or her own writing

- is able to create an agenda for revising.

- engages in self-reflection

- internalizes revision repertoire and chooses techniques from it purposefully

- understands the qualities of good writing and is able to recognize them in his or her own writing

- can use mentor texts independently

- is able to direct writing conferences (for example, brings three endings and discusses which one is strongest)

- can revise independently

## Determining What to Teach Based on What You See Students Doing

FIGURE 2-2

| IF YOU SEE THIS: | YOU CAN TEACH THIS: |
| --- | --- |
| No attempt to revise | Understanding the purpose and power of revision; using simple strategies for revising |
| Some self-correction of conventions | Seeing the difference between revision and proofreading; working on uses of punctuation |
| Sentences that do not follow each other | Focusing and organizing; planning before writing; talking with partner to say more on a topic |
| Lots of scribbles, crossing out, false starts | Planning before writing; rehearsing sentences before writing |
| Ripped-up papers | Having faith in self and writing; saving all work for another time |

memoir, so it makes sense to add dialogue, but it might not fit if she were writing a science report. And beyond that, adding dialogue is not a random choice writers make because it is something they know they can do; it's a deliberate decision. While there is a range of knowledge in the classroom, Connie decides that it is not sophisticated. She also notes that there is a range in willingness to revise. Teaching some specific revision strategies, such adding a short description, choosing a stronger action word, or adding what a character was thinking, may yield results for her reluctant students. Offering concrete, purposeful strategies to use right away will help all the students.

Connie also decides that she needs to teach them that writing must matter personally. Because many students ask to leave the room and lose their focus during writing, she wants to establish that writing workshop is a special, almost sacred time for them as writers and as a community. Based on her observations, this is what Connie decides to do early in the school year:

- teach routines for workshop and review the writing process.

- make it clear that writers have intentions and that revision helps them achieve those intentions.

- focus on three simple revision strategies for early success: stretching out a line of writing to say more, adding in something a character was thinking, and choosing at least one new and interesting word to use.
- call together a small group for intensive work on revision willingness. These students need the support of the teacher and each other to change their attitudes toward revision.
- plan frequent small celebrations of revision successes to highlight the importance and value of revision.
- read aloud published books by mentor authors as models for good writing.
- read aloud teacher-made texts and discuss how the author might revise. This will establish the idea that revision is difficult but worthwhile work.

While students are writing, be sure to observe them closely and take notes on what you see (Anderson, in press; Falk, 2000). Here are some behaviors you might observe:

- student rereads writing during composition and when finished
- student uses symbols (boxes, numbers, stars, arrows, and so on) to indicate revisions
- student appears to know at least two strategies for improving writing
- student seems comfortable with revising
- student makes at least one major revision that shows an understanding of revising versus proofreading

If you decide to go this route, do not display or grade the assessment. Rather, use the information it yields for personal instruction-planning purposes. Also, do not spend more than three days on it because it takes valuable time away from launching your writing workshop (Calkins et al., 2003; Davis & Hill, 2003; Ray, 2001). Your observations of students and study of their writing will help you decide what to teach about revision in your next unit of study.

# ASSESSING STUDENTS TO DETERMINE REVISION STRATEGIES FOR A FIRST UNIT OF STUDY

Gathering information about students in September is crucial to effective teaching. One way to do this is to ask students for a quick writing sample without assigning a topic, as Connie Wu did. Remember that you also want to assess your students' ability to find topics to write about. You might encourage them to write about something that happened to them, perhaps something ordinary like brushing their teeth or losing the TV remote. That way students who haven't traveled to Europe or had their hair set on fire will understand that they still have plenty to write about. Observing students' facility with the writing process—especially revising— is critical at this point.

| Assessing Patterns of Revision Needs to Plan Instruction    Gr 3 | | |
|---|---|---|
| **Subject** | **Monday** | **Tuesday** |
| Organization | Jason, Susie  Julia<br>AnnMarie  Stephanie<br>Ajay<br>Matt<br>Freida | #1  Personal Narr :<br>teach timeline plan<br>beg, middle, end |
| Conventions +<br>  Spelling | Ella  Richard  Sam<br>Jason  Wm  Josef<br>Julia  Chris<br>Matt  Emma<br>Susie  Ajay | Begin word work for spelling<br>start Conventions study<br>late Oct |
| Word Choice | Sam  Josef<br>Matt<br>Julia<br>Chris | Small group work 2x/wk<br>to build word knlg |
| Elaboration | Susie  Matt<br>Jason  Sam<br>Julia  Josef<br>Stephanie<br>Richard | Conferences to focus on<br>elaboration -<br>some MLs in Pers. narr -<br>*do a lot in Nonfiction study |

■ FIGURE 2-3

*Keeping a chart like this can help you determine what to teach in a first unit of study.*

Once you have the papers to examine, look for patterns in the types of revisions students made. For example, you might find that many students have few strategies for writing interesting beginnings or for varying sentence structure. This will tell you what they learned previously about revision, as well as the habits they have developed around revising, such as having only one way to begin (for example, asking a question) or writing only simple declarative sentences because they are grammatically safe. Use a chart to keep track of these revision patterns and habits to decide what to teach in the first unit of study. (See Figure 2-3.)

It may help to keep in mind the Northwest Regional Educational Laboratory's, Vicki Spandel's (2001), and Ruth Culham's (2003) ideas on the traits of good writing. This will prevent you from getting lost in details so that you can focus on large matters related to revision. For example, you might categorize student papers according to organizational skills: those with little or no structure; those with a general but ineffective structure; and those with a structure that clearly drives the logic of the writing. Then you might plan for author studies later in the year to highlight how some writers organize their writing, and small-group instruction for those who seem to struggle with basic organizational structures. (See Chapter 3 for more information on the traits of writing.)

# Using Assessment Results to Plan Revision Instruction in the First Unit of Study

Your first unit of study should focus on helping students understand the structures of writing workshop, the basic principles of writing process, and revision strategies you feel they could use. In other words, we launch the workshop by teaching students how to live what Lucy Calkins (2003) calls a "writerly life." Students learn this by keeping a writer's notebook; finding ideas for writing, planning, and drafting a piece of writing (usually a personal narrative); and revising, editing, and perhaps publishing it. (See pages 14–15 for an explanation of steps in the writing process.) For students who are new to writing workshop, this unit provides a good overview. For those who aren't, it's a good refresher. During the unit you should establish routines and expectations for writing workshop, which include being ready to write every day and being able to give and accept feedback. Lessons might include generating ideas for writing, keeping a writer's notebook (Calkins, 1994; Fletcher, 1996), getting the most out of writing conferences (Anderson, 2000), and establishing a safe environment for writing (Peterson, 1992).

Once students have drafted their pieces, plan on teaching revision strategies. Your observations and notes about students' bank of revision knowledge will help you decide exactly which strategies to teach. For some classes, you will begin very simply, showing them how to add a word using a caret or change dull words such as *nice* to vivid ones. But in many classes, particularly in upper grades, you will be able to move forward quickly and teach them strategies that are more sophisticated. Choose one strategy and concentrate on it: adding more to one line, adding what someone said or thought, changing the beginning, or slowing down one moment and writing more about it. By avoiding teaching too much too soon, you're more likely to establish a positive attitude toward revision. (See Figure 2-5 for strategies to consider.)

FIGURE 2-5

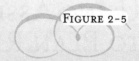

# Simple Revision Strategies:
# Why and How Writers Use Them

| REVISION STRATEGY | WHY WRITERS USE IT | HOW TO USE IT |
| --- | --- | --- |
| Stretch a line, phrase, word | • To make something more important<br>• To make it clearer<br>• To tell readers what it is or what it is like | • Make a picture in your mind to see more of it<br>• Think of the definition of what you are writing about<br>• Use adverbs or adjectives to describe something |
| Add a line of dialogue | • To break up large chunks of writing, making it easier to read<br>• To make a character seem real<br>• To add credibility to your story<br>• To move the action along | • If you were your character, imagine what you would say at that point of your story *or* try to recall what the person really said if it's a true story by playing the movie in your mind<br>• Say the line aloud to test if it's something people really say<br>• Think of words your sibling or friend would use and put them in<br>• Put an X on the spot where you think talking should go, then scout around all day for words you hear that might sound good there<br>• Look in a book to see how a line of dialogue looks when written |
| Revise the beginning | • To grab the reader's interest and lure the reader to continue reading<br>• To reveal some information that is important to story | • Begin with a question addressed to the reader that provokes thought, not a "yes or no" question<br>• Begin with a character talking or a quote that is captivating<br>• Reread and cut early exposition; begin in the middle of the action |
| Eliminate unnecessary phrases and words | • To tighten writing and make it clearer for the reader | • Take out words that bog down writing: *very, like, that, lots of*<br>• Take out phrases that slow down writing: "I am going to write about…," "so that's why…," "now you know the story of…," "my name is…"<br>• Take out long descriptions of places and people and replace them with one or two words that point to the idea; also avoid long descriptions of the weather |

## Conferring to Assess Student Writing and to Determine What to Teach

One of the cornerstones of the writing workshop is the writing conference. Here, teachers meet with individual students and occasionally small groups to provide one-on-one instruction tailored to students' needs. Carl Anderson (2000) tells us that a conference is a conversation with a purpose and a predictable structure that shows students how much we care about them as writers and that teaches them something about writing. A conference is not a time to check up on kids; rather, it's a time to provide targeted, precise teaching. We must always remember Lucy Calkins's (1994) admonition to "teach the writer, not the writing." Anderson (2000) tells us that if we fix students' leads for them or add brilliant dialogue, they will never learn to do it themselves. He tells us that we must "give them the opportunity to learn what we've taught so they can use the strategy or technique for the rest of their lives." I always tell students that if the coach takes the bat from them and hits the ball, they'll never learn to get a base hit on their own.

We get to know our students well through conferences, which gives us information to drive our curriculum. Teachers who confer regularly meet with each student weekly, which means that each student gets to sit with a writing coach up to thirty-five times a year! Imagine how much that young writer will learn.

The benefit to us is that we can assess their writing on the spot. We can see firsthand what students have learned and what they need to learn about revising. Remember that our goal is to create independent writers who know how to revise their own writing.

Information from conferences can inform our whole-class teaching. For example, if we see that a number of students stray from their topics, we can plan and carry out a string of revision mini-lessons about finding a focus and staying with it. On the other hand, if we see that only one or two students are straying, we can continue to work with those students individually in conferences. Keeping careful records of conferences helps us to plan our curriculum for the writing workshop. (See Figure 2-6.)

| Writing Conferences Week of Jeffrey | | |
|---|---|---|
| **Wednesday** | **Thursday** | **Friday** |
| 2/4/04 beg. feature article study → reread NB underline 3 poss. topics for FA | 2/12 topic: lions  FA → need more research call expert: zoo, vet revise plans w/ adding facts (Rev) | 2/24 draft done  FA → study beg. of 3 F.A. texts name wh. authors do — try 3 beginnings in NB (Rev) |
| 3/3  FA → choose 1 or 2 best quotes + eliminate the others (Rev) | 3/9  FA → add voice by using some sent. fragments as if talking — see mentor text (Time for Kids) (Rev) | 3/16  FA → prepare FA for pub by looking at mentor text — add illustration and caption (Rev) |
| 3/25 begin poetry study → reread NB underline poetic phrases + words | 3/29  Poetry → planning: why is this topic important to you? use windows to heart, eyes, etc to help refine idea | 4/6  Poetry → decide on mentor poet in NB, list 3 things you notice from mentor poet * do quick check in 2 days (Rev) |
| 4/8 draft done  Poetry → try 2 things from mentor poet in your poem (chose white space + alliteration) (Rev) | 4/20 wrote 5 poems  Poetry → revise 3 poems for white space + alliteration choose 1 more language element to study (Rev) | 4/26  Poetry → reflect on what learned about poetry plan to take one poem and change to another genre |
| 5/3 begin Realistic Fiction → plan: give character a serious problem bef. you draft | 5/11 drafting  R. Fic. → try writing the ending first so don't run out of writing energy — know ending before begin draft (Rev) | 5/17  R. Fic. → try to tell more ab. char's feelings thru what character does — don't write "He felt sad." Write: "He felt tears in his eyes." (Rev) |

FIGURE 2-6

*Keeping conference records like this one helps you pinpoint students' needs and plan instruction accordingly.*

# CARRYING OUT THE FIRST UNIT OF STUDY

While the entire unit of study takes three to four weeks to complete, you should set aside three or four days for the revision portion of it. Write these days on the calendar, sending a clear message that you have made time to revise and therefore the students will all do it.

Set the stage for revision by discussing how authors may have revised early drafts of published books. Specifically, read aloud several carefully chosen picture books, even if you teach upper grades. Picture books often contain writing that is gorgeous, as well as compelling themes that spark excellent conversation among students of all ages. Some schools even have a book-of-the-month program in which teachers read aloud one title to their students to build school community and encourage conversation across grades (Harwayne, 2000).

To spur discussion about revision, focus students' attention on a part of the book where the author's intention is clear—for example, a part where he or she builds tension or gives us information the main character needs but doesn't have. I would suggest reading one text aloud several times, so students become familiar with it and can look beyond the plot toward the writing itself. Looking back at a picture book is a good way to demonstrate revision strategies, since the books are short and therefore won't overwhelm students.

# What to Teach in the First Unit of Study

As mentioned earlier in the chapter, the first unit of study should focus on helping students understand the structures of writing workshop, the basic principles of writing process, and revision strategies that you feel they could use, based upon your early assessments. For this to happen, obviously, students should begin producing writing at the very beginning of the school year. Many teachers choose personal narrative because they find that writing from experience is easiest for students, but any genre will do. The important point to remember is that, in this first unit, you're not teaching genre. You're teaching structures, principles, and basic revision strategies. Genre studies should begin after the first unit. Here is an outline for a first unit (Calkins et al., 2003; Davis & Hill, 2003; Fletcher & Portalupi, 2001) that spells out general teaching goals and goes on to explain topics you might teach each week.

## GENERAL TEACHING GOALS

- Conduct daily read-alouds from a variety of genres.

- Establish a meeting time during which you teach mini-lessons on writing.

- Expect that students will write for an extended period each day, starting with about ten minutes and gradually moving toward no fewer than 30 minutes.

- Create routines for getting and using materials, for conferring, and for reducing the noise level during writing time.

- Establish a risk-free environment for writing (Calkins, 1994; Peterson, 1992), one in which all students' ideas are valued and respected, and sharing writing with others is an accepted part of each day.

## SPECIFIC TOPICS YOU MIGHT TEACH

**WEEK ONE (after three days of assessment):** Often the product in this unit of study is a personal narrative; however, you might offer students a choice of genre and adjust your teaching accordingly. The main purpose is to teach the steps of the writing process, not the genre of personal narrative. These steps are as follows:

- find a writing identity or the conditions that help each writer do his or her best (for example, I need a quiet place, a clean legal pad, a blue pen); help students say what they need to write
- find a place and time to write every day and establish a plan for writing outside of school
- introduce and have students decorate their writer's notebook (Fletcher, 1996, 1999)
- build a class chart for ideas about what to put in one's notebook
- share entries written in class and at home
- reread one's notebook regularly to get ideas for other entries

**WEEK TWO:** Continue writing in notebooks and add the following:

- reread notebooks to find ideas or an entry that could work as a longer piece of writing
- choose a topic to write about from the notebook (each student will write about his or her own topic, often in the form of a personal narrative)
- plan out writing (for example, with personal narrative you might recall what happened and create a timeline; with fiction you might imagine what could have happened and make a timeline)
- do research by looking at photos, interviewing people, or looking up facts (for example, what is summer weather like in Kansas?)
- write a draft

**WEEK THREE**

- complete the draft
- begin revising and continue revising for four days; earlier assessments will dictate which revision strategies to teach (see pages 47–53 for possible revision lessons)

**WEEK FOUR**
- edit for spelling and other conventions
- publish and celebrate
- reflect in writing on what students learned and could learn next

In the first unit of study, strive to accomplish the following:
1. Teach the steps in writing process and the procedures of writing workshop.
2. Assign students a personal narrative (or other genre of choice) so that they have an authentic task.
3. Teach revision strategies within the context of writing those narratives, choosing strategies based on earlier assessments.

## Revision Strategies to Teach During the First Unit of Study

In the first unit of study, keep the revision strategies simple and direct, so students can experience immediate success with them. This will establish faith that revision is something worth doing.

Here are four revision mini-lessons based on *Night in the Country* by Cynthia Rylant that I've conducted with great success as part of a first unit of study. *Night in the Country* is a short nonfiction picture book that lists what happens during a country night in the summer. I have used it in grades 2 through 8 because there is so much to teach from it, such as writer's craft, organization, and literary elements. Before using *Night in the Country* to teach revision, read it aloud to students so they are familiar with the story. From there, consider teaching the following revision strategies over four days, if they dovetail with the results of your early assessments.

There is no night so dark, so black as night in the country.

In little houses people lie sleeping and dreaming about daytime things, while outside — in the fields, and by the rivers, and deep in the trees — there is only night and nighttime things.

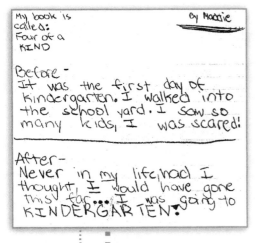

My book is
called:
Four of a
KIND                    By Maddie

Before -
It was the first day of
kindergarten. I walked into
the school yard. I saw so
many kids, I was scared!

After-
Never in my life had I
thought, I would have gone
this far... I was going to
KINDERGARTEN!

*Revising a first sentence to make a strong statement*

---

Ernie

**My first sentence was –**

I fell off my bick and my leg was bleeding.

**I revised it when I was thinking about sound to be-**

When I flipped and fell off my bike, my leg blistered and bled.

**My second sentence was-**

I told me brother he pushed me.

**The sound revision was –**

I tried to tell my brother that Michel pushed me. But I was crying and crawling too much.

*Repeating a sound several times*

## STRATEGY 1  *Beginning with a strong opinion*

**TEACHING POINT:** Read the book's first sentence aloud: "There is no night so dark, so black as night in the country." Most teachers agree that this is a strong opinion that lets us know exactly how the author feels. Rylant is not worried that city dwellers might disagree with her, or that country dwellers might dispute the light of the moon. She feels strongly and states it, and she lets us know what her book is about. Writers, especially nonfiction writers, sometimes say what they want readers to know right at the beginning of their writing.

**STUDENT WORK:** Revise the first sentence of your writing to make a strong statement about your topic that lets readers know where you are headed.

## STRATEGY 2  *Paying attention to the sounds of words*

**TEACHING POINT:** Explain to students that when Rylant wrote the opening sentence, she paid careful attention to the sounds of words. Notice how she repeats the "n" sound three times in the sentence (*no, night, night*), and the long "o" sound three times as well (*no, so, so*). Writers think deeply about the ways words sound and often put words together based on sound.

**STUDENT WORK:** Look for places in your writing where you can repeat a sound several times, and revise accordingly. Don't overdo it, though, because it could wind up sounding silly!

## STRATEGY 3 · *Giving details in groups*

**TEACHING POINT:** Tell students that presenting details in groups often helps with reading comprehension and gives the writing a satisfying rhythm. For example, Rylant gives us three details (i.e., "in the fields, and by the rivers, and deep in the trees") to define the word *outside*, in this passage: "In little houses people lie sleeping and dreaming of daytime things, while outside—in the fields, and by the rivers, and deep in the trees—there is only night and nighttime things." As readers, we sometimes need specific details to clear things up for us. For example, for me, *outside* means "under the streetlamp, by the fire hydrant, next to the deli" because I live in a city. So by telling me exactly what she means by *outside* using three specific details, Rylant helps me to understand. She also creates a lovely rhythm.

**STUDENT WORK:** Find a place in your writing where you can add three details to clarify meaning.

*Grouping details to clarify meaning and create rhythm*

## STRATEGY 4 · *Using punctuation to highlight important information*

**TEACHING POINT:** Point out to students how Rylant uses punctuation to tuck in those three very important details that define the word *outside*. The dashes before and after the details help us to know how to read them. This is one way writers call attention to key parts of the text.

**STUDENT WORK:** Find a place in your writing where you can use dashes as a sign to your reader that you are going to tuck in information. Then add the information.

*Using punctuation to call attention to key parts*

# Demonstrating Revision Using Cynthia Rylant's Strategies in Mini-Lessons

Demonstrating how we can apply what we learn from a writer to our own writing is a powerful way to teach. You can teach the four strategies described above by using your own writing. First, I show students my notebook entry on an overhead transparency. Then I show them a draft that emerged from that entry. From there, I present "revision try-its," or quick attempts at applying the strategies that Rylant uses—one on each of four subsequent days.

NOTEBOOK ENTRY:

> August 4, 2002. Java made another mess yesterday. I'm sick and tired of his shenanigans. I love him so much, but he is so bad. He broke Tina's screen door and went into her house. Then he ate some food and sat on her couch. She's so mad at me over it, but I just don't know what to do. I can't defend him and I have no excuse for not noticing that he opened the gate and ran away. He opened the gate! He is just too smart for his own good and bored living here. He needs police work or seeing-eye work to keep him busy! What am I going to do with him?

DRAFT:

> Java is my brown dog. He is always getting in trouble. I don't know what to do with him. The neighbors complain all the time. One neighbor won't talk to me anymore because he broke into her house and ate her candy. Maybe I should tie him up or find him a new home.

## REVISION TRY-ITS

( STRATEGY 1 ) *Writers sometimes begin with a strong opinion to tell the reader what the writing is about.*

TRY #1   There is no dog so mean, so angry as Java, my chocolate Lab. (Deliberately using Rylant's sentence structure from *Night in the Country*.)

TRY #2   My vet once told me, "Never get a chocolate Lab. You won't sleep for ten years." (Using a quote from an expert to express a strong opinion.)

TRY #3  If I had to do it all over, I never would have let Java in the house. (Reflecting on events I haven't told the reader about yet.)

TRY #4  I should never have let Java in the house. (Shortening Try #3.)

(STRATEGY 2)  *Writers pay attention to the sounds of words when they write.*

TRY #1  Java flies forward, crashing into the cats and clattering into the wall. Then he sits up, slightly dazed, amid cat claws and fur tufts. (Using consonant sounds, single-syllable words, alliteration, onomatopoeia, and assonance.)

TRY #2  In the night, narrowed evil eyes peer out from the pantry. (Using only alliteration and assonance.)

(STRATEGY 3)  *Writers sometimes give details in groups.*

TRY #1  He is always getting in trouble; he digs up flowers, empties garbage cans, howls all night. (Using the present tense.)

TRY #2  One neighbor doesn't talk to me anymore. She's still angry about the day he broke into her house through the screen door, ate the candy on her coffee table, and fell asleep on her couch. (Using the past tense.)

TRY #3  My vet warned me about Java. "He'll ruin your house, your family life, your health," Dr. Marty said. If only I had listened. (Embedding details in a quote.)

(STRATEGY 4)  *Writers use punctuation to highlight important information.*

TRY #1  Java makes trouble—digging up flowers, emptying garbage cans, howling all night—for me and for the neighbors. (Emphasizing Java's bad deeds.)

TRY #2  She won't talk to me about them—the broken screen door, the eaten candy, the soiled couch—but I know she's still angry at me. (Emphasizing the neighbor's concerns.)

TRY #3  The vet interrupted me. "This dog—this nasty, ill-mannered, uncontrollable dog—will ruin your life," he warned. (Emphasizing Java's characteristics within a quote.)

Demonstrations like these give students concrete ways to revise, without overwhelming them. Students can try them and get quick results. And if they see

## Revision Strategies We've Studied

- Zoom in and write about a small part of your story
- You can explain something by adding an example or describing what it looks like
- Add what a character is thinking or doing
- Rewrite your beginning so it's strong or shocking
- Start in the middle of the action
- Write about one thing
- Add dialogue
- Work on using punctuation to make dialogue easier to read
- Make the dialogue sound like the character's personality
- Think about the way words sound together

FIGURE 2-7

*Students created this classroom chart of revision strategies in October.*

results, they're more likely to do more. They come to trust revision. Posting a chart like the one in Figure 2-7 and updating it periodically will help students recall revision strategies long after the lesson is over.

## More Ideas for Revision Mini-Lessons Based on *Night in the Country*

Based on the first page of Rylant's book, I chose four mini-lessons (Ray, 1999). Here are several others I might have taught, depending on my students' needs:

- Writers pay attention to the rhythms of sentences. Two things they particularly notice are word choice (sound and numbers of syllables) and cadence (Angelillo, 2002; Fletcher, 1999; Ray, 1999). For example, Rylant deliberately creates emphasis in the first sentence through repetition and omission of the conjunction *and*; she uses repeated prepositional phrases to create rhythm.

- Writers balance long and short sentences; they use simple declarative sentences when they want to emphasize points.

- Writers use punctuation to help readers navigate long sentences (Angelillo, 2002).

- Writers of nonfiction texts often take a stance and write from a particular angle. They do not just "spit back facts." So when students are writing nonfiction, have them think about how they feel about the information they are covering. Then take a stance and write from that angle (Fletcher & Portalupi, 2001).

- Writers often make broad statements and then take us inside and show us more about them. They tuck in information in order to clarify what they mean. This is one way to teach children to elaborate.

- Writers sometimes explore ideas by presenting extremes, thereby giving the reader a full range of information, such as daytime versus nighttime things (Ray, 1999).

- Writers sometimes embed a definition inside their writing, using a dash to set it off.

Remember that starting slowly with simple strategies, which you carefully choose based on assessment results, builds student confidence. Over the course of the year you will deepen students' knowledge about and skills in revision, but in the beginning, it is best to build their confidence.

## Other Revision Strategies to Consider Teaching in a First Unit of Study

- Change weak words to strong words. Have students start a section in their notebooks where they can collect strong words they hear or read.

- Avoid using too many adjectives, adverbs, and superlatives. Show students how to use more precise nouns and verbs.

- Use dialogue purposefully and genre appropriately. Be sure students realize that dialogue must reveal character and push a story along.

- Change general, overused words such as *nice* and *good* to specific, more original words.

- Be able to state what the piece is really about and stick to it.

- Make writing longer: add to important parts, stretch out time.

- Make writing shorter: take out unnecessary details or events.

- Eliminate long descriptions. Find one or two revealing things to say that capture the essence of what you are describing.

# Summary

Revision work must be based on assessment of student work, so that our teaching is informed and tailored to student needs. In the first unit of study, we should set students up for success by focusing on minor ways to improve writing quickly. We should also establish that revision is a regular and vital part of writing workshop. Students should learn simple, though not simplistic, revision strategies early in the year, and know that living with an expectation for revising is the way they'll approach their writing and learning throughout the year.

## Some Points to Remember

- Model revision strategies using your own writing.

- Use high-quality, familiar literature to model each strategy you teach.

- Break down a strategy into small parts and name how the writer worked with each.

- Ask students to try out the strategy in their notebook entries, their drafts, or both.

- Post a reference chart of revision strategies you have taught.

- In conferences, ask students to name the strategies they use, exact places they use them, and why they use them.

- Refer to familiar literature in conferences as well as mini-lessons.

- Read children's literature to increase your bank of texts.

# CHAPTER THREE

# READING LIKE A WRITER AND STUDYING MENTOR AUTHORS

I n autobiographies by or interviews with authors, invariably they mention some other author who influenced their writing. I know that I've learned so much about teaching writing from reading Lucy Calkins, Katie Ray, and Ralph Fletcher. And I know that the voices of Annie Dillard and Anna Quindlen are in my essays, while the cadences of Toni Morrison and Jacqueline Woodson inhabit the fiction I write. The truth is that learning from other writers—learning to read as they do and studying their techniques—is a fundamental concept. It is an important skill to teach to young writers, because it can have a powerful influence on writing. Katie Ray (1999) tells us that reading like a writer and studying authors changes our teaching and writing forever. It is the key to making students into independent writers, writers who no longer have to ask you, "Is this okay?"

In this chapter, I look at ways to show students how to do this, by discussing authors who may serve as mentors for students and offering mini-lessons on reading like a writer.

# READING LIKE A WRITER

I love going to the theater with my good friend Al, who is an actor. While I notice what most people would as well—how engrossing the story is, how lovely the sets are, and how well the actors perform—Al sees a hundred other things. He notices tension between the actors, he sees little slips that escape me, he talks about the preparation behind the performances, blocking, timing, voice, truth. Al sees more because he is trained to see more.

Writers read the same way that Al watches a play. When writers read, they see more than an interesting story. They see craft, structure, tension, character development, foreshadowing. They notice all the things that make writing an art. Writers read with eyes that notice the writing behind the story. Just as Al analyzes a fine performance onstage, writers analyze a fine performance on the page.

Most of us do not read this way. We read for enjoyment or to learn something new. When we finish a piece of fiction, we may discuss the plot and the characters. When we finish a piece of nonfiction, we may discuss the facts and what they mean to us. But rarely do we talk about the writer's technique, unless he or she does something so unusual that it jumps off the page to annoy or surprise us. Unless we are professional writers, we don't usually notice the writing. This is a good thing, because it enables us to just sit back and enjoy the text. Good writers make writing look easy. But a lot of work goes into making it look easy, and that's what writers know how to spot.

It is so powerful to teach students to read like writers. By showing them how to *notice* what writers do and how they write, you open a world of study (Fitzgerald, 1989; Ray, 1999; Schwartz, 1990). Never again will they be "finished" with a book; they can go back to any page and dig to find the writer at work. They can use what they find to figure out how to revise their own writing.

Reading a book only for enjoyment is not reading like a writer, although writers certainly enjoy what they read! Rushing through a book to get to the end is not reading like a writer, either. Reading like a writer means *slowing down*. With fiction, it's best to read through a book—even a picture book—first, to get the story. This enables the reader to know what happens at the end, and may even prompt him to talk about the plot and characters for a while. Then the reader reads the book again to look at the writing itself. From there, he may read it many more times, because it is only in getting to know a text well that he is able to see through to the writing. Professional writers practice this regularly, so they can often spot a writing technique on a first read; students, however, need some teaching and time to practice. In this section, I show you how to do that.

The writer Richard Peck (1992) says, "No one but a reader ever became a writer." When I mull over this remark, I think that we can extend it to "No one but a reader ever became a reviser." So much of knowing what to revise hinges on having a sense of how a text was created. Students who read fluently or who have texts read to them frequently have more of a sense of story structure, how words sound together, the rhythm of language, and so on. They can, for example, sense that when description

is getting too long, it will be broken up. They can hear how writers tuck actions into dialogue. They can appreciate the rhythm of sentences, the precision of a perfectly placed word, or a change in pace. For these students, revising comes smoothly. For others, we must make these aspects of good writing visible. We must read to students every day, particularly if they are not deeply literate, to make them hear the music of well-crafted texts before we ask them to write and revise.

## What Readers See When They Read Like a Writer

They see how writers

- structure their writing

- begin and end their writing

- maintain the reader's interest

- build in tension

- introduce and reveal character

- make their characters interact

- use dialogue to move a story along

- convey facts in an interesting way

- combine words and visual imagery to help the reader understand a concept

- use techniques such as questioning to make the reader wonder about the world

- honor and use words carefully and precisely

- make readers hear their unique voices

FIGURE 3-1

## Things You Might Point Out When Reading Any Piece of Writing Like a Writer

- I notice how the writer gets me right into the story by starting in the middle of the action.

- I notice that the writer started with a compelling piece of dialogue that gets me into the story (for example, the first line of *Charlotte's Web*: "Where is Papa going with that ax?").

- I notice the writer started with a good question—not a "yes" or "no" question—that gets me wondering.

- I notice the writer uses short sentences with one-syllable words to make the scene move fast and feel tense (for example, Gary Paulsen's *Hatchet*).

- I notice the writer mixes short and long sentences and, by doing so, creates a rhythm.

- I notice when the writer chooses to put words with the same sound all in a row.

Reading like a writer should not be relegated to a separate unit of study, but rather embedded within *every* unit of study. It will make learning writing and revision easier for your students, because you'll have so many writers out there helping you teach. In fact, I would introduce the concept in the very first unit of study by pointing out things writers do, particularly as I read aloud to students. (I might also point out things they *don't* do, such as write "The End" to close their pieces!) Getting students reading like writers early on prepares them for subsequent units of study in which they study mentor authors to find revision techniques.

At the beginning of the year, plant "casual statements," such as the ones listed in Figure 3-1, within your read-alouds to provoke thought about more than just the book's story line and raise awareness about reading like a writer before you even begin to teach. Some students will pick up the concept and run with it, but most will need direct instruction. The following mini-lesson will help.

## An Early-Year Mini-Lesson on Reading Like a Writer

It's important to teach students early in the year to study texts. A good way to do that is with this mini-lesson. Start by choosing a text that is familiar to students—one that has been read aloud to them perhaps—so they are not focused solely on "getting the story." Put a portion of the text on overhead transparencies or a chart.

With her fourth graders, Lisa Schofield likes to use Ralph Fletcher's *Flying Solo*, which is the story of a group of students who teach themselves one day when their substitute teacher doesn't show up. This short novel helps the class to bond and creates many opportunities for discussion. Lisa reads it once for students to understand and enjoy the story—purely for the reading experience. From there, they read it again with an eye toward determining what Fletcher does well as a writer. Lisa encourages this behavior—listening for different purposes in read-aloud—all year. She finds that it helps students realize that good writers take time to compose carefully and deliberately. Many of her students return to Fletcher to uncover ideas for revising.

Here is one of Lisa's first mini-lessons on reading like a writer using *Flying Solo*. Notice that she follows a very careful sequence of steps, which helps her students grasp ideas and gradually make them their own.

## INTRODUCTION OR CONNECTION TO PREVIOUS LESSONS

Writers, I know that most of you are completing your first drafts of your personal narratives, and you are ready to do some revising. We have a few revision ideas that we wrote on the chart, which you can use to get started. (See Figure 2-7.)

But last night I had another idea. I looked back over *Flying Solo* because I love that book like you do. Ralph Fletcher is an amazing writer and he really spoke to all of us in that book. So I began to wonder what I might learn about revision by studying his writing. Could I learn something about writing from him? So I reread some of the book looking for big and little things that Fletcher does as a writer. Today I'm going to share something that I noticed with you.

## DEMONSTRATION

[*Lisa puts the following passage from* Flying Solo *on the overhead projector and reads it aloud to the class.*]

"Helen Pierce had been the school secretary for nearly thirty years but had never gotten used to the frantic pace of the mornings. She took a sip of coffee and closed her eyes, trying to think. There was a nagging splinter in her mind, some-one she was supposed to call, something she had to do, but what? Who?" (p. 32)

Well, the first thing I want to say is, Ralph Fletcher is such a good writer that I could study him for years and always learn new things about writing. In this passage, I notice something he does that you may want to use as a revision strategy.

Right here, Fletcher uses the words *nagging splinter* to tell us that something is on the character's mind. Now, it won't help me just to copy those same words—after all, that would be stealing from him. Instead, I can think about what Ralph Fletcher did and why. He wants us to know that something is bothering the character, so he's written about something that bothers *us all*: splinters. He's chosen just the right word to for us to understand exactly how the character feels. Now I know that when I want to describe how a character feels in one my own stories, I can search for just the right word.

## ACTIVE ENGAGEMENT

Now I would like you each to look over the first page of your draft. Find a place where you want to let us know what a character is thinking or feeling, and talk with a classmate about how you might do what Ralph Fletcher did.

[*After giving students a minute or two to look over their drafts, Lisa crouches beside two pairs of students and listens in on their conversations. From there, she continues the whole-class lesson.*]

Okay, let's come back together. When I was listening to some of you, I heard interesting things. I heard one person say that he wants to make his reader understand that he was disgusted by touching a live fish, but simply saying "It was slimy" isn't good enough. So he's going to read some books and look through his word lists to find alternatives that might make readers understand just how disgusting touching the fish was. Then he'll try several words in his draft to see which ones work best.

## ASSIGNMENT OF THE DAY'S WRITING WORK

So your work for today is to reread your entire draft and find at least one place where you can change a word or use a comparison to help your reader understand you better. After you've done this in your draft, please reread your writer's notebook and practice it on an entry or two. Use what we've learned from Ralph Fletcher as a revision technique to make your writing stronger.

[*In subsequent days, Lisa teaches two more revision strategies that she found by studying Ralph Fletcher's writing: telling what that character is thinking, and using a repeated phrase of dialogue to reveal character.*]

# Revision Strategies Inspired by *Flying Solo*

FIGURE 3-2

| WHAT RALPH FLETCHER DOES | HOW LISA TRANSFORMS IT INTO A REVISION STRATEGY |
|---|---|
| Uses little description and exposition. What's there is used judiciously to move the story along | Take out description or explanations that slow the story down |
| Tells most of story through dialogue | Add dialogue; make sure each line moves the story forward |
| Ensures dialogue sounds like real people talking | Read dialogue aloud to "hear it"; ask peers to read it; does it sound like real people talking? |
| Uses dialogue to reveal character | Match each line of dialogue to the characters' personality traits; consider sparing use of colloquial phrases when appropriate |
| Provides a main character that the reader gets to know deeply | Examine the story to see if one character is drawn from many angles, and other characters support that character's story |
| Presents big ideas inside an interesting story; there is a surface problem, but a deeper problem, too | Reveal deeper ideas within the ongoing action (in exposition, dialogue, characters' thinking) |
| Alternates dialogue and actions so the reader "sees the scene" when characters talk | Imagine the scene in your head and write stage directions for the characters within the dialogue |
| Uses metaphors to help the reader get inside a character's head | Give characters something to do or be fascinated with that will show readers what they're like |
| Uses dialogue tags such as "he said" only when needed to help the reader follow the conversation and not in the same position in every sentence | Remove some dialogue tags and include action to clue in reader to who is talking |
| Uses italics to highlight thinking, dialogue from the past, definitions of words, personal writing | Use a change of font or italics to indicate thinking or something from the past |
| Uses time markers such as "an hour later" to move the story along | Indicate the passage of time, even without giving exact time |

Although there are many revision strategies that Lisa can teach based on Fletcher's work, she teaches only a few at a time because she doesn't want to overwhelm her students this early in the year. (See Figure 3-2 for a list of possibilities.)

It is interesting to note that each item in Figure 3-2 can be deconstructed and expanded. For example, "Uses dialogue to reveal character" can become a study of exactly how Fletcher does that: He uses phrases or fragments, the way real people do when they talk. He gives characters trademark phrases, which are repeated in the book. There is no useless prattle. He avoids using dialogue tags other than "she said" or "he said," which enhances the flow. When young writers are able to articulate how something is done, they can then do it themselves.

FIGURE 3-3

## How Writers' Actions Can Help You Meet Your Teaching Goals

| TEACHING GOAL | HOW WRITERS MIGHT DO IT |
|---|---|
| How to build a story | Give a character a significant problem<br>Write smooth transitions to keep readers interested<br>Balance narration and dialogue |
| How to start a story | With a clever observation by the main character or narrator<br>With an important statement by the main character or narrator<br>With an unusual question<br>With a statement of belief |
| How to build tension | Withhold information<br>Use short words in short sentences<br>Tell important parts of the story<br>Let the reader know things the character doesn't know |
| How to use language effectively | Pay attention to the sounds of words<br>Choose precise words |
| How to build realistic characters | Give them good and bad traits<br>Make them talk truthfully<br>Show their actions<br>Let them solve their problems<br>Tell us what the main character is thinking |
| How to end a story | Make sure the problem is solved<br>Set up the ending at the beginning |

At this point, Lisa's class studies Fletcher to see how much they can learn from one writer. Lisa introduces this important concept, which she will extend later in the year with a mentor author study. After showing students how to find answers to writing questions by looking at what authors do, give them the opportunity to look in books—any books—to practice the skill on their own. Make a two-column chart of their writing questions and the answers they find. As time goes on and students begin to compose and revise based on what they notice writers do, add a third column to the chart with examples of student writing that show the strategy in action. This model for learning how to revise by studying writing will serve you and your students all year, in every unit of study (Hansen, 1991; Murray, 1993; Ray, 1999).

This may be a new way to teach for you. If so, give yourself some time to reorient yourself. And don't give up. In my experience, it is the best way to teach students to revise. If they can study writers and use what they find to revise their own writing, they will be well on their way to becoming independent, confident writers themselves.

## Texts That Help Students Read Like a Writer

Rather than hunting down hundreds of books, choose a few very fine texts, also known as mentor texts, that lend themselves to teaching revision strategies—books that are extremely well crafted and will stand the test of time. Read mentor texts aloud several times so students get to know them well. Choose them with the class, because if students are to learn from them, they need to love them as much as you do. Here are some suggestions for mentor texts to get you started, but keep your eyes open for others. There are hundreds more out there. I'll look at the concept of teaching from mentor texts more closely throughout this book.

*A Day's Work* by Eve Bunting, Clarion, 1994.

*All the Places to Love* by Patricia MacLachlan, HarperCollins, 1994.

*Amos and Boris* by William Steig, Farrar, Straus and Giroux, 1971.

*Come On, Rain,* by Karen Hesse, Scholastic, 1999.

*Henry Hikes to Fitchburg* by Donald B. Johnson, Houghton Mifflin, 2000.

*Miz Berlin Walks* by Jane Yolen, Philomel, 1997.

*Night in the Country* by Cynthia Rylant, Bradbury, 1986.

*Owl Moon* by Jane Yolen, Putnam & Grosset Group, 1987.

*Smoky Night* by Eve Bunting, Harcourt Brace, 1994.

*Snow* by Uri Shulevitz, Farrar, Straus and Giroux, 1998.

*Snowflake Bentley* by Jacqueline Briggs, Houghton Mifflin, 1998.

*The Other Side* by Jacqueline Woodson, Putnam, 2001.

*The Quiltmaker's Gift* by Jeff Brumbeau, Pfeifer-Hamilton, 2000.

*The Whales* by Cynthia Rylant, Scholastic, 1996.

*Tough Boris* by Mem Fox, Harcourt Brace, 1994.

*What You Know First* by Patricia MacLachlan, HarperCollins, 1995.

The overarching belief here is that it's better to just choose a few books and use them to teach a lot about writing. Picture books are effective because they are short, but using selected pages from chapter books is equally valuable. The key is for students to care about the text and know it well.

Our goal should be getting students to use mentor texts on their own. We want to move them toward relying on many texts by the same author—in other words, to help each student discover a "mentor author," someone from whom the student can learn many things about writing across many texts.

## The Importance of Learning from Masters

In his book *Write to Learn*, Donald Murray tells us that writers read in special ways. They notice graceful, effective writing and study what authors do to accomplish it. Writers study other writers the way musicians study other musicians and ballplayers study other ballplayers. In fact, in any area, one should study the masters to learn how to improve.

Students need to know that they can learn much from writers, and that studying texts by those writers is a powerful way to do that. When Carl Anderson was writing his book *How's It Going?* (2000), he referred constantly to Ralph Fletcher's *What a Writer Needs* (1993). Day after day, he returned to Fletcher's book for "advice" on how to start a chapter, how to organize information, and so forth. That book became Carl's mentor text, and Ralph Fletcher became Carl's mentor author. Without even talking to Fletcher, Carl learned so much from him. We need to show students how to do that using their own mentor texts and authors.

# STUDYING MENTOR AUTHORS

Once students have been introduced to the idea of learning to read like writers, the next step is to teach them to study one writer for a long time and in a deep way. This is akin to apprenticing themselves to a master, and it can be accomplished on an ongoing, informal basis and/or as part of more formal author study, described later in the chapter.

Everything from cooking to blacksmithing and from acting to writing is learned this way. Ideally, every classroom should have a living, breathing writer in residence. Every child should have a personal writing coach, whom he or she chooses from all the published writers in the world. Obviously this is not going to happen, so he or she must do the next best thing: study a mentor author's texts and imagine the choices that author made and why.

Student writers can learn to do this. Once they know how to read like writers, they can find authors they love and spend lots of time reading, studying, and thinking about those authors' books. It's not important that the authors write about topics the students like, although that can initially spark a student's interest. What's more important is that the *writing itself* matters to the student and will teach him or her how to write and/or revise. The main thing we need to do is teach students how to notice and apply the writing techniques authors use.

Some teachers use mentor authors as a way to teach students to think about, plan, and draft their writing, but we can also use them to show students ways to revise their writing. We want students to look at texts to get ideas for ways to change their own writing. Here are some questions writers might ask when studying a mentor author:

- How did the author structure this piece of writing, and how can I do the same thing?

- What are some craft choices this author made, such as word choice and sentence rhythm?

- How did the author allow his or her personality to show through the writing?

- What is the purpose of this writing and how did the author convey that to me?

- What is the genre of this writing? Why did the author choose it?

- How did the author elaborate on his or her topic or theme?

- Where is the writing especially clear, and what did the author do to make it that way?

Each time a writer asks one of these questions, he or she should also ask these next two questions and transfer answers to his or her own writing:

- Is this something that can help my writing?

- How and exactly where can I apply it in my writing?

Deep study of mentor authors is powerful because it gives students a tool for writing independently. No longer will they feel frustrated and lost if they haven't had a conference with you. They can pick up any text—long or short—notice and name something the author has done, and try it in their writing. Studying both the composing habits and finished work of authors provides students with sound advice (Bannister, 1993).

The next step is for students to understand the purpose behind what writers have done. This way of reading is more sophisticated, so it takes time for young writers to master it. At first, they will notice something they like, and they will try it in their own writing again and again, devoting little thought to the effect it creates. In some ways, students are "playing around" with writing, and it's an important step. Peterson (1992) tells us that "play enriches the imagination, provides opportunities for developing originality, and strengthens the individual's ability to cope with problems and the unexpected." Children need time to just play around with writing (Heard, 2003; Ray, 1999), the way young sculptors might play with clay and young basketball players might dribble balls for hours. Eventually these artists and athletes become more skilled and purposeful, and so will young writers. Young writers will come to understand that they can look for writing techniques from their mentor authors but that the techniques must be used purposefully. So the writer may start by trying some alliteration because she found it in a Karen Hesse book but will eventually become a fluent writer purposefully using alliteration to create a certain effect and help her reach a particular goal. In other words, she stops "copying" mentor authors and starts applying their techniques when she needs them. Each learned technique may become part of her repertoire of writing skills. Of course, it is up to us to help students make this cognitive

**Mentor Author** May 15
Joanna Kamien

I chose Karen Hesse for my mentor author because after I read her book Out Of The Dust I liked the way she mixed sadness and hope.

I like to write sad things, especially poetry, so I decided that when I wrote a historical fiction story I would do it like Karen Hesse did, with so much sadness, but at the end, so full of hope. But the thing I like most about her stories is that you think you know the true meaning, but as you read it again and again you start to find hidden meanings you couldn't find the first time. I wanted my story to be like that.

Ms. Scofield told me that a story written in poetry form/style was one of the hardest to write, and I was up to the challenge.

In preparation for this kind of writing I read Out Of The Dust over and over, until I felt I was ready, and I think I accomplished this task with my story *True*.

### True

By: Joanna Kamien

I feel all alone in the world.
Fear grasps me.

I see mother,
Rocking back and forth
On the hard, wooden bench,
Holding little Baila,
And silently singing,
Shana medalah,
Shana medalah,
Pretty girl,
Pretty girl,
I pray she will survive,
That all of us will survive.

I clutch my cat Tova,
Her orange fur brushing my face,
As the train rolls on,
To Dachau.

The pretty fields I could once see
Are now blurs of color.
I shiver
In my tattered clothes.

Father says to me,
"Joseph, do not be afraid"
But I am afraid,
Afraid I'll die.

I look at the Nazi soldier
Standing
Almost frozen

In the corner.

The other passengers
Look scared, sad, lonely,
Pulled from our homes
To die.

*August 1943*

We have been in the concentration camp
For three weeks now.

Mother has burns
Red, big,
She never stops crying.

She hides Baila
In her bed
Of thin blankets
So the people won't kill her.

I do the same with Tova,
And I pray they won't find her.

Father tries to remain calm,
But I can tell he is burning inside.
He aches for home.

Being the age of 11,
I work too.
I try to act grown up,
But secretly,
I cry at night.

Every day
There are less people
In our bunk.

*A fourth grader reflects on using a mentor author and applies what she's learned in her own poem.*

leap; one way is through author studies (see below) and another is an advanced revision study (see Chapter 8). Throughout the year we will encourage students to consider these goals while we confer with them.

# Getting to Know Mentor Authors Through Author Studies

Author studies are an effective way to teach students a great deal about both reading and writing. In any author study, the class studies one author together, or, in some cases, each student chooses his or her own author to study. There are many facets to author study, and you should read Laura Kotch and Leslie Zackman's excellent book on the topic (Scholastic, 1995). For the purposes of revision, we can use author study to show students specifics about the author's writing and then have the students use them as revision strategies.

Begin the study by choosing a mentor author, someone whose writing the class loves (Kotch & Zackman, 1995). Be sure the author writes in a variety of genres and across several reading levels, so that everyone in the class can find texts with which he or she feels comfortable. On the other hand, if all of your students aren't ready for long texts and/or multiple genres, you might want to start with poetry (Flynn & McPhillips, 2000) to teach the basic principles of studying authors and then move on to picture books, chapter books, and young adult novels.

During the study, read the author's books aloud, keep bins of the books in the classroom library, write selections from author's writing on charts and sentence strips and display them in the room. Do this so you have the author's writing to refer to in conversation, to surround students with the author's words, and to highlight sections you will use in instruction. In order to support the idea of revision, ask students to imagine how the author works through the writing and revising process. Find interviews with the author in magazines, book club flyers, and online; use these to build class knowledge of the author's life and how it supports his or her writing, as well as to find information about the author's writing or revision routines. This information helps students build a full picture of how an author works.

You should schedule an author study sometime before the winter holiday break. That will allow students enough time to feel comfortable with writing workshop but will also leave time to mine the work for later revision. Teachers often do author studies based on fiction writers, and this is profitable. But given the emphasis on nonfiction reading and writing in education today, I recommend doing author studies with nonfiction authors as well. Some teachers will do author studies twice, once in the fall with a fiction author and once in the winter or early spring with a nonfiction author. (See Chapters 4 and 5.)

## Good Choices for Author Studies

| | |
|---|---|
| Avi | Angela Johnson |
| Eve Bunting | Patricia MacLachlan |
| Sharon Creech | Katherine Paterson |
| Christopher Paul Curtis | Gary Paulsen |
| Roald Dahl | Patricia Polacco |
| Kate DiCamillo | Cynthia Rylant |
| Ralph Fletcher | Gary Soto |
| Patricia Reilly Giff | Jerry Spinelli |
| Kevin Henkes | Jacqueline Woodson |
| Karen Hesse | Jane Yolen |

# Reading and Writing Concepts
# to Teach in Author Studies

**In reading, we can teach students the following concepts:**

- Authors write from the events and interests of their lives.

- Authors have certain themes that recur in their writing.

- Authors make decisions about which genre matches their purpose.

- Authors have craft techniques and literary devices they use repeatedly.

- Authors have similar characters and/or settings in their books.

- When you understand an author's style, you can read his or her books more easily.

- When you like an author's work, you read expecting him or her to write a certain way. For example, I expect Gary Paulsen's books to be about wilderness adventures, to have lots of suspense and sparse language.

- When you know an author's work well, you can begin to think like that author. You might wonder, for example, what Patricia Polacco would say about a certain issue.

**In writing, we can use the following questions to teach students to use what they know about an author to plan, compose, and revise their own work:**

- Based on what you know about your mentor author, how can you find ideas for writing from the events and interests of your life? How can you live your life more like that author to create the circumstances that will give you more to write about?

- What are the big ideas or themes that you think about? How can these ideas find their way into many of the stories you write, and into your writing across genres?

- Do you consider writing about something in many genres, or exploring it from many different angles to see which is the most precise, powerful, or thought-provoking? How can you do this?

- What craft techniques do you use? What else can you learn about craft from the mentor author? How can you embed that into your writing without merely copying the author's work?

- What characters have you created and why? What settings do you know well enough to write about with authority, or how can you learn about other settings so thoroughly that you can convince us you live there?

- What characteristics in your writing make it familiar or easily identifiable to readers? How can you develop those qualities?

- What can you do as a writer to make your reader comfortable? How do you use words and conventions to ease your reader's journey?

- What else can you learn from your mentor author in terms of writing, such as structure, tone, mood, use of story elements, use of dialogue, and so on?

- How can you revise your writing based on what you've learned from this author?

## PLANNING AN AUTHOR STUDY

Here are some points to consider if you decide to carry out an author study:

- Clarify in your mind exactly what you want students to learn about reading and writing from this author; consider the qualities of good reading and writing.

- After one to two weeks of reading texts by the author, add in notebook writing where students write their observations about the author's work, try out some of the author's writing techniques, and make plans for a longer piece of writing that will reflect the author study.

- Provide a variety of texts by the author at several reading levels.

- Use one text for whole-class study and other texts by the same author for small groups or partnerships.

- Provide supporting information about the author: biography, memoir, interviews, reviews of books.

- Assign writing about the reading, as well as personal writing in which the students apply the author's techniques (Angelillo, 2003).

- Plan celebrations such as sending letters to the author or reading the author's work aloud to senior citizens or to children in hospitals.

# Sample Mentor Author Studies

It's important to see this work in action to understand it completely. So here I explain how two gifted teachers carry out author studies.

## SIXTH GRADE

Tina Colangelo teaches sixth grade at Canton Intermediate School in Canton, Connecticut. Every year she does a mentor author study with her students on Kevin Henkes. Although Henkes's books are simple storybooks created with younger children in mind, Tina feels that his themes, messages, and writing techniques are sophisticated enough for eleven-year-olds. This is wise, because studying a long novel in depth would be difficult for her sixth graders. Tina uses Carol Jenkins's ideas about author study as multiple response (1999), including interacting with the text to extract meaning (Rosenblatt, 1994). (See box on page 72.)

One of Tina's goals is for her students to understand that even a simple text may contain sophisticated writing techniques they can try. While her students eventually write literary essays on the themes in his books, they also use Henkes as a way to study revising. Eventually they look for Henkes's writing techniques in longer books. Having studied simple texts helps them to recognize craft in longer writing.

Tina begins the study by reading aloud one of Henkes's books, *A Weekend with Wendell*. The class talks about what it notices about Henkes's writing and makes a chart together. (See Figure 3-4.) In the days that follow, students search

| What we saw in Kevin Henkes's writing | Example from *A Weekend with Wendell* | Examples from our own writing |
|---|---|---|
| Purposeful repetition | "Soon," said her mother. "Soon," said her father. | "Let's go," Mom said. "Let's go," Dad said. "Let's go," I said. |
| Problem revealed on the first page | "Oh boy!" said Wendell. Sophie didn't say anything. | On the first day of camp, I knew my bunkmates hated me. |
| Events organized in groups of three | They played house, hospital, bakery | We went hiking, fishing, and swimming. |
| Careful attention to sounds of words | Weekend with Wendell | I flew fast down the stairs. |
| What characters don't say | Sophie didn't say anything Sophie said to herself | "Who did this?" Dad asked. I didn't answer. |
| Characters with different personalities | Wendell always acts crazy; Sophie feels left out. | Whenever I eat pickles, my brother makes a face and pretends to throw up. |
| Time markers | On Friday afternoon…, On Saturday morning…, At lunch…, At bedtime… | The next morning I couldn't go to school. |
| Change in situation and character | Sophie takes over. Sophie decides she likes Wendell after all. | Jeremy decided he wouldn't fight with Matthew anymore. |

FIGURE 3-4

*A sixth-grade class created this chart based on what it noticed about Kevin Henkes's writing in* A Weekend with Wendell.

other Henkes books to find those traits and to discover others. Then they attempt the same strategies in their own writing.

Finally, Tina asks the students to join book clubs in which they read chapter books by either Jerry Spinelli or Katherine Paterson. Although it is challenging for them, the students read these books looking for the same qualities they've seen in Kevin Henkes. For example, Spinelli and Paterson each reveal a problem early in their stories. They use time markers and build change into their characters. Students conclude that many writers use similar techniques. These lists become possible revision ideas for student writing.

## Theories of Author Study

Carol Jenkins's work (1999) synthesizes much of the thinking about author study during the 20th century. Author study may be approached as *literary biography*, which focuses on studying the interplay of the author's life and works, with the author at the center of a literary experience, and on allowing the student to see writing as a mirror of his/her own suffering. On the opposite end of the spectrum is the theory of *critical response*, which regards literature as a self-contained and autonomous act. According to this theory, reading is a critical and objective dissection of work and a search for ambiguity, paradox, irony, structural attributes, literary qualities, and layers of meaning, and no attention is given to the author's life or reader's response. Another view is *reader response* theory, based on Louise Rosenblatt's transactional theory (1994), in which a text becomes a text only when a reader brings experience, attitudes, and values to the work. The primary reason for reading an author in this way is to engage in response.

Jenkins advocates a theory of author study as *multiple response*, in which readers respond in multiple ways to an author's works, and which includes elements of all three of the approaches above. Aesthetic engagement must precede critical and biographical response; critical response deepens and extends literary experience (for example, teaching literary elements such as symbolism, point of view, plot, character development, and theme); and biographical response heightens and intensifies literary experience. The author is seen as a person and a writer. Keeping Jenkins's ideas in mind helps teachers create rich experiences for students during author studies.

## THIRD GRADE

Barbara Rosenblum does an author study with her third graders at PS 6 in Manhattan every winter. This year Barbara and her students studied Cynthia Rylant. When I visit her class in the spring, she is investigating ways to build independence in her students by reviewing and extending the concept of that study. Barbara's students each choose their own author to study. Specifically, she is going to have her students study their chosen authors to find ways to revise their own work. Barbara always wants her students to become independent writers, so she asks them to think about their own writing compared to their mentor author's writing.

Maddie
Adding in a story
Before: Dad just walked away from us because he gave us a timeOut!

After: Dad just walked away from us because he gave us a timeout! My dad always gives me timeouts for nothing. Once he gave me a timeOut for putting scotch tape on a broken lock! Really–a broken lock!

**FIGURE 3-5**

*A third grader tries the strategy of incorporating a story within a story.*

Their assignment is to list three techniques they notice in their mentor author's writing and then to revisit previous notebook writing to try those techniques as revision strategies. Barbara asks them to label their revisions "before" and "after," so they can demonstrate how trying an author's technique changes and improves their writing. Their celebration at the end of the study includes students reading the "before" and "after" sentences and explaining the technique they tried. (See Figure 3-5 for a student sample.)

You may want to teach revision as part of a whole-class study, as Tina did, or to take your cue from Barbara by studying a single author at the beginning of the year and having students choose their own authors later in the year, focusing on revision. Deconstructing writing this way is powerful. Students watch you do it with the whole-class mentor author and then see what they can learn from their own mentor authors. Once they've found things their author does, they can revise for a long time, trying to perfect those things by doing them again and again. Revising is not a chore when it involves discovery and play, and when we give students ways to figure out how to do it. Author studies lead to independence because they give students tools for revising without relying on us.

# A Day-by-Day Plan for Teaching Revision within an Author Study

Here is a template for a possible author study on Eve Bunting, angled toward teaching revision. Remember, the key word here is *possible*—you might need to expand or delete part of it, depending on your students' needs. We pick up the study in progress, at the point where students have already spent a week or two studying Bunting's life, themes, and craft, and drafting their own pieces of writing. So the students are prepared to revise their drafts in writing workshop.

## DAY 1

**TEACHING POINT:** Writers learn to organize their writing by studying the organization of their mentor authors' writing.

**MINI-LESSON:** When I look at my mentor author, Eve Bunting, I see she organizes her work in several ways. One way is that she sets up a situation, and then the rest of the story is a series of events that flow from that situation. She does this in *Going Home* and in *Fly Away Home*.

So as a revision strategy, I'm going to make sure that all the events in my story come directly from the main situation I set up in the beginning.

## DAY 2

**TEACHING POINT:** Studying the organization of mentor authors' writing leads you to plan a better ending for your own writing

**MINI-LESSON:** When I look at the endings of Eve Bunting's books, I notice that they are not neat. They don't always make me think that everything will be all right. The endings of *Smoky Night*, *Going Home*, and *Someday a Tree* are all hopeful, but they don't make me feel like the story is over.

In my own story, I notice that I tried to make the ending perfect, as if everything would be fine from then on. So now I think I should revise it to show that there is hope that things will be better, but that life isn't always perfect.

**DAY 3**

**TEACHING POINT:** Writers use words in new and surprising ways.

**MINI-LESSON:** One thing that surprises me about Eve Bunting's writing is that she uses unusual combinations of words. For example, she uses describing nouns and adjectives that don't seem to go together, although they work well. In *A Day's Work*, she writes "huddled silence" and in *Swan in Love*, she writes "silvery laughs." This makes her writing original and interesting.

So I am going to read through my draft to see if there are one or two places where I might use some unusual and descriptive words, and then I'm going to work in my notebook and write interesting combinations.

## Some Revision Strategies to Teach Inspired by Eve Bunting

| TITLE OF BOOK | REVISION STRATEGIES |
|---|---|
| *Going Home* | ORGANIZATIONAL STRUCTURE: list of events that brings main character to a new understanding about life<br>THEME: grows from a character's observations of a new situation |
| *A Day's Work* | ORGANIZATIONAL STRUCTURE: story's problem leads to complication, which leads character to learn an important lesson<br>VIBRANT VERBS: "truck cruised along," " throat burned with tears"<br>SURPRISING ADJECTIVES: "huddled silence"<br>THEME: grows from a mistake a character makes |
| *Fly Away Home* | ORGANIZATIONAL STRUCTURE: list of musings that ends with character's hopes |
| *Smoky Night* | ORGANIZATIONAL STRUCTURE: bigger problem introduced, then brought into character's life<br>METAPHORS: cats fighting, then holding paws in fear<br>THEME: grows from a real-world event |
| *Someday a Tree* | ORGANIZATIONAL STRUCTURE: story with problem and hopeful resolution<br>VIBRANT VERBS: "moonlight whitens my room" |
| *Swan in Love* | SURPRISING ADJECTIVES: "silvery laughs," "starlit wind"<br>THEME: is actually stated early by a character's voice |

These lessons show the depths we can reach in an author study. Knowing the texts by mentor authors well makes it easier for students to understand the complexity of the revision strategies we teach.

In case you have any lingering doubts, I give you this example. Lisa, a sixth grader, studied Karen Hesse and read *Come On, Rain!*; *Out of the Dust*; and *Witness*. At the end of the study, her teacher asked Lisa and her classmates to write a list of writing "truths" they had learned from their authors, which they could use when composing or revising their own work. This is Lisa's list:

- Choose a deeper problem to hold up your story, preferably one that others can relate to, such as the tensions between mothers and daughters. You can write about that problem again and again in different ways.

- Show what a character is thinking by what he or she does, like tugging on her hair to show she's nervous.

- Only describe what the reader needs to "get" the story—leave out the extra stuff that's nice but you don't need it.

- Use strong verbs and nouns—read books looking for cool words and write them down.

- Don't tell obvious things, but work them into the story through character's actions and reactions—leave out lots of description.

- If you need something to happen at the end, make sure you plant a way for it to happen earlier in the story.

- Make your characters smart by the way they solve problems, manipulate the situations and people around them, and by the way they treat others.

- Use words carefully: think about their sounds, their rhythms, and what they mean when they are put together with other words.

- Move your story to a breaking point or place where the character makes a change—try to make your language be its best at that point.

- Use short words in a row to build tension.

- Write your ending long and deep so the reader has a sense of relief and completion.

# SUMMARY

Teaching students to revise means more than giving them lists of ways to make their writing better. To make students understand the power of revision, teach them to read like writers and to study authors. Author studies are important for many reasons, including learning about revision. As we study authors and then look at our own writing, we become filled with ideas for making our own writing more professional.

## Some Points to Remember

- Students need to be shown how to find possibilities for revision by examining texts.

- Reading like a writer involves developing a sense of what writers do to make their writing strong.

- Writing is not a casual act; there is thought, planning, and purpose behind it.

- Students should read looking for writers' techniques, and then use those techniques while composing or revising.

- Teachers should use mentor author studies to demonstrate how to read like a writer and how to learn from a writer.

- To become independent, students must find mentor authors for ideas on how to revise.

# CHAPTER FOUR

# STUDYING STORY ELEMENTS AND MENTOR AUTHORS TO REVISE FICTION

I sit beside Tommy during writing workshop one dismal, cold November morning. The gray sky hangs low outside the window. Tommy's mood matches the weather. He's yawning, rubbing his eyes, and avoiding rereading or revising his paper. Aside from the obvious question about the amount of sleep he had the night before, I wonder if anything else is bothering him. So I ask, "Is there something that's keeping you from writing?"

Tommy shrugs. "I don't know what to write," he complains. "I've got to fix up my story, and I don't know what to fix."

Composing and revising realistic fiction presents difficulties for many students. They begin writing with little planning and get lost in plots that go nowhere or everywhere. The freedom to "make it all up" sometimes translates into "having no boundaries," and as a result students end up writing fantastical tales of witches and dragons that end, all too often, in blood, guts, and death. Not very realistic. Students like Tommy benefit greatly from the writer's maxim "write what you know," although they also benefit from, as the writer Richard Peck (1992) points out, writing about what they can find out. Learning to construct stories based on events from their lives grounds students in reality, and studying how authors craft their stories gives them years of writing and revising material for their stories.

Teaching young writers to view the small events of their lives—the subway ride to school, skateboarding in the schoolyard, cleaning up after a puppy—as ideas for stories about *someone else* is liberating, because they don't have to struggle to make it all up. When they tell their stories in the third person, the stories sound new, exciting, and original. While some predictable problems arise when doing this— inevitable switching from third to first person, putting in excessive or irrelevant detail, and closing with pat endings ("And then we went to bed. The end")—it is nevertheless an effective way to build fiction-writing skills. And since the stories are based on real events, students can more readily find ideas for revision.

When we teach fiction writing this way, students learn firsthand how and why *elements of story* (plot, setting, character, change, movement through time) make sense (See Figure 4-1.) In fact, these elements are considered so key to reading and writing fiction that some states, such as Connecticut and New York, test for understanding of them in their reading and writing assessments.

So in this chapter, I examine how to help students write realistic fiction using elements of story and ideas from their lives, while teaching them concrete revision strategies using mentor authors.

FIGURE 4-1

# The Elements of Story and Implications for Revision

## PLOT

This is the series of important events that make up a story. Ansen Dibell (1988) tells us that plot is "a way of deciding what's important and then *showing* it to be important through the way you construct and connect the major events of your story." She advises writers that there has to be something of value at stake— "something of value to gain or…to be lost." In other words, plot drives everything characters say, think, feel, or do in a story. "Struggle, conflict, dissatisfaction, aspiration, choice" are the basis for effective plots. William Noble (1994) tells us there must be drama or confrontation of some sort.

**Implications for Revision:** Students determine whether there is "something of value" at stake, and whether it drives their characters. They look for the confrontation or conflict, and decide to what extent it controls the story.

## SETTING

This includes not only "the physical backdrop of the tale, but the historical background and cultural attitudes of a place and time,…[and] the mood of a time" (Bickham, 1993). In some cases, as in historical fiction or ethnic or culturally based stories, it includes how the people talk. It is important to help students understand the difference between setting and scene: a story is set in North Carolina in the 1960s and moves through *scenes* in the kitchen, the schoolyard, and the beach.

**Implications for Revision:** Students determine whether they have established a strong setting for their story, and understand that if they don't, readers will assume the time is now and the place is "anywhere USA," even if that is not their intention. When revising, it is helpful to state the setting and reread to be sure it is kept consistent. Students may also revise to weave setting throughout the piece.

## CHARACTER

Most stories hinge on one main character, and writers work hard to make readers care deeply about what happens to that character. There often is a "supporting cast" of other characters, but each of them appears mainly to advance reader understanding of the main character and to push his journey along. Writers develop characters through the ways they think, talk, and react to situations and other characters. Robert Newton Peck (1983) claims that readers (and TV viewers) really remember the characters writers create—for example, we remember Ramona, Charlotte, and Harry Potter more than the details of what happens to them.

**Implications for Revision:** Students reread to determine if the main character is strong, consistent, and believable, if the supporting cast truly supports the story, and whether the characters have their own personalities. They may need to return to notebooks to do more planning.

## CHANGE

Change may happen in the circumstances of the character's life (character convinces family to move away from bullies) or, more effectively, in some quality inside the character (character finds strength deep within him that helps him to deal with the bullies).

**Implications for Revision:** Students find the point of change in their stories, and determine where they have planted information to make the change plausible. If no change has taken place, they plan major revisions to include one.

## MOVEMENT THROUGH TIME

Stories most often happen across time, whether it is an hour or several years. Noble (1994) writes, "Stories play *against* time, creating conflict and a springboard for things to happen and for a rising uncertainty."

**Implications for Revision:** Students trace the movement through time in their writing, considering not only the time markers they've used ("an hour later"), but also how effectively they've skipped time (we don't need to know everything) and used it to build suspense by slowing or hurrying the action.

# Using Elements of Story to Drive Revision

Once you have taught students to read like writers and use mentor authors to build revision skills, it's important to get them applying those skills as quickly as possible to the genre you teach. Let's assume that you have scheduled a unit of study on realistic fiction sometime in late fall. I recommend two major goals for the unit: get students studying published examples of high-quality realistic fiction to discover the features of the genre, and have them use those texts to find ideas for revision.

## Format for a Unit of Study

Here is a typical format for a unit of study on writing realistic fiction.

### STUDYING PUBLISHED EXAMPLES

As in any other unit of study, begin by employing Brian Cambourne's principles of learning, which are described in Figure 4-2, and *immersing* students in texts (Cambourne, 1991). Students need to read many good examples of the genre and of the kinds of materials they will write. Therefore, for a unit on writing realistic fiction, you should have a number of picture books or age-appropriate short story collections available that contain *the kinds of stories you expect your students to write.* (Avoid including historical fiction in this study; while the stories are realistic, the term *realistic fiction* implies setting in the present time.) While many students will also read realistic fiction chapter books during the study, use picture books at this early stage because they are shorter and easier for students to handle from beginning to end. The purpose is for students to begin to recognize and talk about the elements of story and how they contribute to understanding a story.

Choose a read-aloud text by a mentor author. You will use this text as the basis for many of your lessons, so be sure it has many of the features students should notice—a clear plot with a problem and resolution, setting described through exposition and dialogue, characters that are strong and unique, some change in the situation or characters, and a clear timeline of the events.

Once students have discussed the features of realistic fiction found in the immersion texts, make a chart of what they've noticed and use the read-aloud

FIGURE 4-2

# Cambourne's Principles of Learning Applied to Revision Studies

## IMMERSION

Students read many texts and discuss their features. Choose texts for genre, author, or use of writing techniques. Long and short texts are included, as well as articles, picture books, and the environmental print. In this phase, students become thoroughly familiar with the kind of text they are going to study.

## DEMONSTRATION

The teacher demonstrates revision strategies that come from the texts by using artifacts or actions. He or she thinks aloud, helping students make meaning from the demonstration.

## EXPECTATIONS

The teacher communicates positive expectations of success for all students. Students understand they are all expected to revise their writing.

## RESPONSIBILITY

The teacher allows students to have some choice in what they will write, or which revision strategies they will use, in order to help them become independent learners and decision makers.

## APPROXIMATION

Students attempt to copy the adult model, whether it is the teacher's demonstration or a technique they discovered in their mentor author's writing.

## PRACTICE

The teacher provides ample time for students to practice these developing revision skills.

## ENGAGEMENT

Students engage with the author's texts and the teacher's demonstrations. They must feel capable of doing what is taught and assured their revision work will be accepted without ridicule as they try new skills. This principle is critical, because true learning cannot take place without student engagement.

## RESPONSE

Students and teacher exchange thoughts and clarify points during lessons and conferences. Exchanges must be relevant, honest, nonpunitive, and readily applied to the revision work at hand.

---

text to clarify or extend their understanding of these elements. You may find that students are unclear about the features of realistic fiction and will not be able to name the elements of story. This is where you can use the read-aloud to scaffold their thinking by steering the discussion toward these elements. Then you can direct students to look for these elements in chapter books they read, as well as to think about using them to write stories.

## FINDING STORY IDEAS AND BEGINNING TO WRITE

Ask students to search their notebooks for story ideas, especially ones that come from their own life experiences. Teach mini-lessons on how to identify life experiences that make good stories, and how to alter details of those experiences to make them more dramatic. Students must give their characters a problem: "the day the girl went to the park" is not a story until they alter it to "the day she went to the park *and got lost.*" Another key piece for young writers to understand is handling time. So your lessons may include how to make timelines of events and use them to plan a story, how to choose which part of a story to tell (rather than the entire event), and how to use phrases to move time along.

Another way to help students mine their lives for story ideas is by having them play "What If?"—a game in which students fill out a three-column chart on their initial story ideas, based on life events, and note why each event won't work as a story as it happened and what they will need to do to transform the event into an effective story. This helps students to imagine other possibilities for their experiences. (See Figure 4-3 and Appendix D for a reproducible version of this chart.) Students can fill out the sheet on their own or in small groups, before they begin drafting, to help them revise. Even students who have lots of notebook entries on life experiences may have trouble isolating one for a story, so always be on the lookout for these students and work with them in individual conferences or small groups as necessary.

## BEGINNING THE REVISION WORK

Once students have planned their writing and drafted, begin the revision work. As always, what you teach in revision depends on your ongoing assessment of your students' needs. (See Chapters 2 and 10 for ways to assess students.) Since one of the larger goals of teaching students to write fiction is to teach them the elements of story, we'll likely base most of our revision lessons on those elements as well. I've found that teaching story elements in a series of lessons helps students on many levels. It builds knowledge of this very important aspect of fiction; enables them to use that knowledge as they revise their work; and addresses many individual needs that I discover through assessment, such as not understanding the nature of a problem, or that it must be solved at the end, or that characters are individuals. In other words, teaching story elements yields big results in a relatively short period of time.

| My Idea from My Notebook | Why It Won't Work | What If...? |
|---|---|---|
| My birthday party | Nothing big happened. It was fun. | nobody shows up<br><br>the candles go on fire<br><br>I have a fight with my brother |
| Going to the country | Who cares that I get carsick. No one cares that I threw up. | It's an important drive (to pick up a new dog), and then if I get sick, it will be a big thing. |
| Trying out for baseball | I didn't make the team, so there's nothing to tell | I say how I felt because my dad was angry with me.<br><br>Tell the part of the story about dad and me, not the try-outs.<br><br>Make dad madder than he really was. |

FIGURE 4-3

*A "What If...?" chart allows students to prepare for story writing by playing with ideas from notebooks.*

## Using Story Elements as Revision Strategies: One Teacher's Approach

Karen Perepeluk teaches fourth grade in PS 59 in Manhattan. Her realistic fiction unit comes early in the year because she wants her students to have a strong knowledge of elements of story in preparation for the New York State fourth-grade writing assessment, which is given in January. When she assesses her students this year, she discovers that most of them have a solid handle on plot, character, and setting, but are weak on movement through time and change. In the process, she gently introduces them to movement through time and change in the context of that teaching, planning to cover those elements in more depth later in the term. Since her students are young, most of them only nine years old, Karen expects there will be a lot of revision to do. She decides to limit the work to six days, two days for each of the three familiar elements, building in time for small-group work and conferring on each of the elements. While she begins with only two revision strategies, she adds more as she sees students becoming comfortable applying the initial two in small groups and conferences. (See Figure 4-4.)

## A Mini-Study on Revising Dialogue

In this mini-study, you spend several days studying revising dialogue. You might ask students to highlight the dialogue they've written and then ask them to consider whether it works according to the points below. Each of these points could be a mini-lesson topic, if you feel your students would benefit from the instruction.

- Dialogue moves the action along—something must happen in the dialogue.

- Dialogue must be tight; cut anything that doesn't move the story forward.

- Dialogue should sound like real people talking, even if it's not what real people would actually say.

- Take out any exposition in dialogue. For example, a character would not say, "I'm in the bedroom, Mother, combing my shiny blond hair," which is one way novice writers try to tell readers that she had blond hair.

- *Said* is not dead! Writers use it all the time because it does fine work in helping readers pay attention to excellent dialogue; other tags are often used to prop up weak dialogue. (Read William Noble's wonderful book *"Shut Up!" He Explained* for more information.)

- Use stage directions to help the readers know who is speaking.

- Limit the number of tags.

- Write dialogue that moves between two people and be sure their lines alternate so readers can keep the conversation straight.

- Reveal character through dialogue by choosing the characters' words carefully.

- Characters must say enough so the dialogue carries the story. One line amid two pages of narrative usually isn't enough, unless the writer has a reason for it. Readers' eyes get tired when there is no dialogue to break up their reading.

- Give some characters favorite lines to say again and again.

- Teach all the many conventions of written dialogue by studying what published texts look like.

FIGURE 4-4

# Karen's Day-by-Day Revision Lessons

## DAYS 1 AND 2: REVISING PLOT

**TEACHING POINT:** Writers give their characters significant problems appropriate to their ages.

**STUDENT WORK:** Imagine what will happen to the character if he or she doesn't solve the problem. Then find a way to tell the readers what that awful possibility is. One way is to weave it in through what someone says to the character.

**TEACHING POINT:** Writers reveal the character's problem as soon as possible in a story.

**STUDENT WORK:** Make your character tell us the problem in the first or second paragraph. (For example, saying "The boat seeps water slowly" in the first or second paragraph will make us read on, expecting it may sink by the end.)

## DAYS 3 AND 4: REVISING CHARACTER

**TEACHING POINT:** The problem must fit the kind of character the writer has created.

**STUDENT WORK:** Give the character qualities that show just how enormous the problem is for her or him. (For example, "The boat is sinking and she can't swim.") Tell your readers this early in the story.

**TEACHING POINT:** The characters must have traits that make each of them unique. Perhaps they repeat a phrase frequently, get teased at school, or cry a lot.

**STUDENT WORK:** Choose something that will make one of your characters unique and weave it into the story. (For example, "She taps her feet when she's nervous.")

## DAYS 5 AND 6: REVISING SETTING

**TEACHING POINT:** Writers let readers know where and when the story is happening.

**STUDENT WORK:** Weave in the information about setting in at least three places by adding short sentences or observations. Do not give a map or exact dates unless they are historical facts. ("Like many of the lakes in Maine, this one was quiet but desolate." "The lake water was warm, and bugs circled her head and sang.")

**TEACHING POINT:** Writers use setting to reveal or amplify the problem.

**STUDENT WORK:** Let your character tell the reader something about the setting in a way that reveals more than what surroundings look like. ("I'm terrified of coves—can't we get snagged on rocks here?")

# Revision Strategies for Elements of Story

Here is a chart of possible strategies for elements of story. Of course, you will find others as you study mentor texts with your students. As always, base your teaching decisions on your assessment of student needs.

| PLOT | SETTING | CHARACTER | MOVEMENT THROUGH TIME | CHANGE |
|---|---|---|---|---|
| Make sure something happens in your story. | Be sure you know the time and place of story and why. | Ask yourself if your characters are believable or like comic-strip characters. | Decide how long the story takes from beginning to end. | Be sure you know the changes that will happen in the story. |
| Name the problem and stick to it. | Don't tell the exact address and date unless it matters. | Make them consistent (always nasty or witty). | Make a timeline for the events and label the time frame of each one. | Check that there are places where you planted clues that a change would take place. |
| Put events in an order that makes sense. | Weave setting into the action. | Choose names carefully. (Use baby naming books.) | Weave time markers such as "an hour later" or "after breakfast" into the story. | Make clear to the reader whether the change is on the outside or the inside of the character. Show inside changes by revealing what the character is thinking. |
| Make sure your ending is believable and effective. | Clarify the general setting for the reader, as well as scene changes. | Know your character—his or her habits, likes, tics, favorite phrases, and so forth. | Check if time markers are consistent. | |
| Avoid trick endings (such as "Then he woke up"). | Don't change the scene too many times. | What does the character want? Add detail to make the main character stand apart from other characters. | Avoid writing exact times and dates unless they are critical to the story. | |
| Develop the middle to prepare readers for the end. | Be sure to tell readers when your characters move to a different scene. | | | |
| Move the story with dialogue. | | Give each character a distinct way of speaking. | | |

# Using Mentor Authors to Drive Revision of Realistic Fiction

In Chapter 3 we looked at the idea of using mentor authors to teach revision; now we will observe mentor authors in the context of a unit of study in realistic fiction. In author studies, the focus is learning how to deeply study an author to learn *anything* about writing from him or her. The focus shifts when the unit of study is a genre of writing—realistic fiction, poetry, feature articles, and so on. When studying a genre, you study authors to figure out *techniques that writers use to write that genre*. The revision strategies you seek grow from the genre—in the case of realistic fiction, they may include how to move from scene to scene, how to use dialogue to show characters' traits, and so on. Whether you look at one or several authors to find answers to writing questions, your questions are related to the genre you are writing. Of course, students must know how to study an author before you ask them to look at one technique across many authors. Furthermore, it makes sense to teach certain concepts within the context of a certain genre, so search for those within various authors' work in each genre. (See Figure 4-5.) The authors' work you study will serve multiple purposes in a genre unit of study.

FIGURE 4-5

## Major Concepts Within Genre Units of Study That Can Drive Revision Decisions

There are major concepts about genre that we teach in each unit of study, such as elements of story in realistic fiction. This chart shows major concepts for four units. You can be sure that you teach those concepts if you plan the school year with them in mind.

| UNIT OF STUDY: | REALISTIC FICTION | FEATURE ARTICLE | POETRY | LITERARY ESSAY |
|---|---|---|---|---|
| Major Concepts: | Elements of story; use of dialogue; sense of rising action; point of view | Organizing and communicating information; understanding audience; writing with voice | Deliberate word choice; organization; rhythm and cadence of language | Exploring an idea or theme within one or more texts; creating and organizing thinking; using text to justify ideas |

Since there is *too much to teach* in any one unit of study, it is important to determine exactly what to teach and which authors will help you teach it. Let's assume that by reading students' notebooks, conferring with them, and assessing early drafts, you've noticed that students do a good job creating a solid problem and solution. But you've also noted some patterns of challenges. Many students, for instance, do not create strong characters or do not use setting to support their stories. Based on this decision about what to teach, choose several authors who fit your needs: they write about very different characters (Polacco, Yolen, Hesse) or use setting as more than a backdrop for stories (Paulsen, Lowry, Woodson).

Perhaps you notice that many students seem to drift easily into imaginary elements—witches and monsters show up in their entries about going to the park with grandmother. Choose authors who ground their work in reality, such as Paulsen, Spinelli, and Christopher Paul Curtis. Or you confer with students and you find that more than half of the class has little sense of story in terms of conflict or content; they tend to write "lists" of events and call them stories. Choose authors who create challenging problems for their characters, such as Mildred Taylor, Patricia Reilly Giff, and Kevin Henkes. Or you read over their early drafts and find that there is little focus on one character, nor is there any attempt to explore that character at all. Turn to Spinelli, Hesse, and Yolen for advice. In addition to looking to authors for instruction for each of the above scenarios, you might decide to do the following activities: separate reality from imagination by making double-sided entries in notebooks or highlighting and deleting any otherworldly events; work on the idea of a "problem" in a story by telling stories orally and then writing the problems down; choose the main character and use the notebook to develop that character's personality.

In any case, identifying what students need in terms of realistic fiction and then finding authors to match that need will give power and substance to your teaching. Use quotes from sections of the authors' work to show students *how* those authors created characters or conflict or whatever you need to teach.

## Draft 1 (handwritten)

Title?

On a cold winter night in ~~NY~~ NYC a 12 year old girl went through the city streets. She signed and watened the cloud of her breath rise up to the roof tops. The wind bit at her bare hands. She shifted the basket on her shoulder.

"Mama!" she cried. "I'm back and pushed open the door.

'Sofia Johanna come in. you shall catch a cold.'

"Mama! I never get sick!" was her reply

"Wher is papa?" she ~~asked~~ added?

## Draft 2 (typed with handwritten marks)

HANNA                    Hanna

Title?

This was originally t in the Middle — Story — moved on own

On a cold winter night in New York City, a twelve year old girl stumbled through the city streets. The icy wind bit her bare hands. She trudged towards the tiny apartment, placed smack down in the very middle of one of the most run-down streets in the city. She sighed and watched the cloud of her breath rise up to the rooftops. She shifted the basket on her shoulder.

"Mama!" she cried. "I'm back!" She opened the door.

"Sofia Johanna! Come in! You shall catch a cold!" cried her mother.

Teehee! she already opened the door!

"Mama!" Sofia cried exasperatedly "You know I never get sick!" ~~as she said this she opened the door.~~ She saw her brothers, Isaac and Heni the building something with in their corner with old blocks even on the building

"Where is Papa?" asked Sofia. she was wiping a dish with an old rag. Sophia recognized

"Oh, he'll be back," replied her mother. Sofia knew she was trying to act calm, but she noted a tone of worry in her mother's voice. it as her fathr old hand kerchie

"Did you get potatoes and bread at the store?" she added, trying to change the subject. Sofia lowered her eyes and said quietly,

's closed Mama."

Sophia could tell that her mother wasn't to lled with this new peice of information.

## Final version

### ~Frozen Tears~

On a cold winter night in New York City, a twelve year old girl stumbled through the city streets. The icy wind bit her bare hands. She trudged towards the tiny apartment, placed smack down in the very middle of one of the most run-down streets in the city. She sighed and watched the cloud of her breath rise up to the rooftops. She shifted the basket on her shoulder.

"Mama!" she cried. "I'm back!" She opened the door.

"Sofia Johanna! Come in! You shall catch a cold!" cried her mother.

"Mama!" Sofia cried exasperatedly "You know I never get sick!" as she said this she opened the door. She saw her brothers, Isaac and Henri building something with old blocks they had found out on the street in their "Play Corner."

"Where is Papa?" asked Sofia.

"Oh, he'll be back," replied her mother. She was wiping a dish with an old rag Sofia recognized as her father's old hand kerchief. Sofia knew she was trying to act calm, but she noted a tone of worry in her mother's voice.

"Did you get potatoes and bread at the store?" she added, trying to change the subject. Sofia lowered her eyes and said quietly,

*A fourth-grade student revises realistic fiction by embedding a character's thoughts and actions in dialogue.*

# A Close Look at How to Overcome Challenges

(CHALLENGE 1)  *Students cannot separate reality from fantasy.*

POSSIBLE SOLUTION: Demonstrate through literature that realistic fiction could happen, whereas fantasy cannot. In this case, the choice of mentor author is tricky. Be careful not to choose authors who blur the lines between fiction and fantasy, either by writing a realistic story in which a fantasy element will briefly appear (Cynthia Rylant, Jane Yolen) or by writing realistic stories in which the characters are animals (William Steig, Kevin Henkes). The text must be exactly the kind of writing you expect the students to write, so you must search for the most realistic text you can find. Good authors for realistic fiction include Patricia Polacco, Katherine Paterson, Patricia MacLachlan, and Jerry Spinelli.

Judy Nadler teaches fifth grade in New York. Her class is writing realistic fiction stories, and she wants them to revise using mentor authors. But some of her students drift off into fantasy when they can't think of good endings or compelling problems for their stories. Judy decides to focus on Patricia Polacco, because Polacco writes about realistic problems, which she never solves with magic.

She calls the students together and asks them if they recall *My Rotten Redheaded Older Brother*, which she has read to them several times. Not only do the students remember it, they smile and murmur about their favorite parts. Judy tells them she likes this book as a mentor text for realistic fiction because the story is very real—that is, a real family has a real problem that is solved in a real way. She says that Polacco resists having anything magical happen—for example, a fairy godmother doesn't come and solve the problem. Then she rereads some parts to them and asks them to listen and think about how Polacco does this.

After they listen, the students talk with their partners. They tell Judy that the situation or problem in the story is similar to problems real children have. Then they look at some of Polacco's other books (*Thunder Cake*; *Thank You, Mr. Falker*) and they realize the same thing happens in those books as well. The class concludes that Polacco writes about real problems children have, and that is why she doesn't have to rely on magic to solve them. They decide that they must examine their stories to see if they've written about real problems, or if they've made the problems so overwhelming that only magic can put things right.

**CHALLENGE 2** *Students do not understand the difference between a story and a list.*

**POSSIBLE SOLUTION:** Choose two texts, one that is a clear story with problem and solution, and one that is a list. Read the first and point out the problem and how all events build to the solution. Keep a chart. Then read through the other, showing that there is no problem, just a list of events. Add this point to the chart. Some text choices for this are *A Weekend with Wendell* by Kevin Henkes or *Thank You, Mr. Falker* by Patricia Polacco for problem and solution, and Cynthia Rylant's *When I Was Young in the Mountains* or *The Relatives Came* for lists.

Barbara Stein teaches third grade in Pennsylvania. Many of her students' stories just go on and on because the students don't know how to distinguish stories from lists when reading. More specifically, her students don't yet understand that stories have a predictable structure that contains a problem, rising action, turning point, and resolution. (For more information on the differences between story books and list books, see the box at right.) This may be because Barbara often reads aloud books by Byrd Baylor to them, which are often "lists" and not stories in the classical sense with conflict and solution. So Barbara decides to focus on another author, Eve Bunting, who writes in a more traditional way. Barbara reads several of Bunting's books to the class (*A Day's Work, Smoky Night*), and asks the students to listen for the central problem. Then they look at other books, separating them into two categories: stories where there is a problem, and stories where there is no problem, only lists of events.

Once the students see the difference, they go back to revise their own stories by adding in a problem. For some students, that means completely changing their story. Barbara feels the work is worthwhile, because she wants the class to understand that a compelling problem is the foundation for constructing plot.

## Story Book or List Book?

Many books that are called stories are actually lists of events. A story usually has a particular format—problem, rising action, turning point, resolution—while a list is just a series of events that may be organized chronologically or in some other way. An example of a story is *Chrysanthemum* by Kevin Henkes, because the character has a problem that seems to get worse until it is resolved. An example of a list is *The Relatives Came* by Cynthia Rylant, because there is not a problem or conflict, just a list of events that happen when the relatives visit one summer. It's okay for students to write "stories" using either structure, as long as they know the difference between them.

## CHALLENGE 3  *Students have trouble creating strong characters.*

**POSSIBLE SOLUTION:** Using a text, make a chart with the students on how the main character is strong, full, and vibrant, with many facets to his or her personality.

Mentor texts should include characters that are strong, and emphasis must be on *how* the writer created them (character has a unique voice, strong or unusual opinions, shows some originality or courage, and so on). Good authors for strong characters are Sharon Creech, Jerry Spinelli, and Jacqueline Woodson.

Sarah Daunis is unhappy that so many of the characters in her fifth graders' stories are bland and boring. The characters all seem to sound and act the same, yet Sarah knows that strong characterization is a key element in story writing. To teach this concept, rather than using picture books, Sarah uses some of the chapter books she's read aloud during the year: *Crash* by Jerry Spinelli, and *Walk Two Moons* by Sharon Creech. Both of these books have a strong, memorable character, which the class has discussed at length.

Sarah asks the students to imagine the work that Spinelli and Creech might have done in preparing to create their characters and make them unique. The students examine copies of the books, looking for ways that each author made the characters stand out. They conclude that Spinelli puts the reader inside Crash Coogan's head to hear what he is thinking about others. They feel Creech also lets the reader hear the character, since Sal's voice is very distinctive. Sal reacts to events and uses everyday language to talk to the reader.

Sarah's students decide to go back to the characters in their stories and revise them by doing three things: write what the characters are thinking, write how they react to events around them, and write more distinctive dialogue that makes the characters feel more real.

In each of these cases, the teacher guides the class to find something within an author's work that helps with revision. Of course, the next step is to ask students to find answers to revision questions by examining authors on their own, and helping them to understand that there are few fiction questions that cannot be answered by studying a mentor author's work. Ultimately, we hope students will gravitate to authors they've chosen on their own for "advice" on how to revise their writing.

## Reflection                    By: Evan

This year I've come very far in writing. At the beginning of the year I wasn't writing seriously. I was writing silly stories such as <u>How I met Chocolate Applesauce.</u>  My teacher Ms. Scofield taught me that I could write seriously if I tried, and when I did, my stories were great.

Looking back to the beginning of the year was funny, seeing how much I've progressed. Writing isn't easy, but it's worth it in the end. Also reading books by my mentor author Gary Paulsen helped me express my thoughts. My first copy is always full of errors, and is sloppy, but it's a start. But when my final copy is done, I like to compare the first, and final copies, to see the big difference.

I have progressed greatly since the beginning of the year, and Ms. Scofield has helped all the way. And trust me, no more applesauce.

*A fourth-grade student reflects on how he's grown as a writer, thanks in large part to studying Gary Paulsen's work.*

# SUMMARY

Including a unit on realistic fiction in your curriculum calendar is important for many reasons. Students develop a sense of story by studying story elements. When we guide students toward finding answers to questions about these elements using books by authors they know and love, we give them a tool for improving their own stories. Choosing mentor authors we refer to again and again is key, although we should always be open to new authors and ideas.

## Some Points to Remember

• Writing realistic fiction stories helps students recognize and understand the elements of story.

• Teachers should identify through assessment which areas students need to focus on in revision.

• Teachers can focus on revising one or all the elements of story, but must teach students how to do it.

• Teaching revision by studying mentor authors builds independence and confidence.

# CHAPTER FIVE

# STUDYING MENTOR AUTHORS TO REVISE NONFICTION

I t is February, and it's raining steadily in Vancouver, British Columbia. I shake off my drenched coat and umbrella and enter Crofton House School, a girls' independent school that is over a century old. In stark contrast to the outside world, it's warm and bright inside.

Susan VanBlarcom's sixth-grade students are meeting with their third-grade partners to revise the math concept books they are writing together. The girls are collaborating on writing and illustrating picture books about mathematical concepts. The books will eventually be used by the first graders at the school. I overhear one conversation: "Should we change this word?" the sixth grader asks. "I don't know," answers her third-grade partner. "What do you think?" I know the teachers place great emphasis on revising, and I am pleased to hear young writers discussing word choice.

However, one third-grade teacher, Jacqueline Heibert, tells me she is concerned. She nods toward the partners talking about words and whispers to me, "I worry that their revision choices are too random. They seem to know a few good revision tricks, but they don't know how to use them wisely." Jacqueline's observation strikes a chord. Yes, the girls are talking about words, but there is little conversation about why they might change a word—for instance, if the one they chose is too

## Planning a Unit of Study in Nonfiction Writing

When we invite students to write nonfiction, we ask them to look at the world around them and to share their knowledge. Chances are they've been doing this for most of their lives, since the time they began writing birthday cards for their parents, lists of presents they want for their birthdays, and rules for the games they play. Because children are naturally curious, they already know a lot from just being alive, and they can teach what they know to others. So from the start it's important to teach them that there is so much to discover, and that uncovering, investigating, and sharing a passion through writing is greatly satisfying.

When you begin a unit of study in nonfiction writing, ask yourself these questions:

- What do my students already know about nonfiction writing? Are there types of nonfiction writing that I know they already write well?

- What qualities of good writing do I want to teach my students through nonfiction? (See Chapter 6.)

- How much time can I allot to this unit? Does my schedule allow me to teach two or three kinds of nonfiction or just one? If just one, which one?

- Is this the only time of the year that I can set aside for a nonfiction writing unit, or can I plan for another unit later in the year?

- Will students write about individual areas of expertise, or should I choose a topic for a shared inquiry, such as animals, the Civil War, or the solar system? If it is a shared inquiry, does my schedule allow time during the day for students to do research? How will I divide instructional time between learning about the topic and writing about the topic (determining categories, organizing information, drawing conclusions, and so on)?

- Do I have materials (books, magazines, Internet access) available for them to collect information?

- How many finished pieces will I expect? For example, could students produce a feature article, a page of reflection on facts they've discovered, several note cards, and a letter to an author as a result of this study?

sophisticated for the audience or isn't precise enough—or about how to find more appropriate words, such as combing through math books and their own notebooks.

In addition to this cross-grade project, Jacqueline and her colleague Laura Hill are in the midst of a nonfiction unit of study with their third graders. So they ask me to work with them on ways to make their students more aware of revisions to nonfiction informational texts and more deliberate in their attempts to make them.

In this chapter, I look at the work of Jacqueline, Laura, and other talented teachers. Specifically I explore how they do the following:

- maximize student learning in nonfiction writing
- study a nonfiction mentor author
- teach students to collect a variety of mentor texts to fit their needs
- cover revision, day by day, within a nonfiction writing unit of study

# How to Maximize Student Learning in Nonfiction Writing

When you think about it, nonfiction is a very large umbrella for many different genres of writing. Some nonfiction is based solely on the writer's experience, some is based on the writer's research, and some is based on a combination of both. (See Figure 5-1.) Regardless of the origin of the information, the writing grows out of a desire to communicate that information to others. In this chapter I examine only the genres of nonfiction writing that are based on research, since I see them assigned most frequently as part of nonfiction units of study in the classrooms that I visit.

There are many reasons for teaching genres of nonfiction writing. Nonfiction requires students to use many higher-order thinking skills, such as remembering, understanding, applying, analyzing, evaluating, and creating—skills in keeping with Bloom's taxonomy (Anderson & Krathwohl, 2001). Reading and writing nonfiction texts raises the bar for student thinking in workshops.

Jacqueline and Laura plan their nonfiction unit of study around writing science-related feature articles, which requires their students to find and learn a lot of new information (Davis & Hill, 2003; Lattimer, 2003). They give their students a choice: The girls can either choose topics on their own to research and write about, or they can choose one inspired by a whole-class science exploration—for purposes of this discussion, the solar system. Allowing choice sends out two messages: first, that writers like to explore a lot of subjects, and second, that interesting writing can derive from content-area work in school. Jacqueline and Laura hope deeply that the girls are so interested in and inspired by the science information they gather that they will want to share it with the world through writing. They want the girls to experience the excitement and curiosity of the quest—the search for information. They also want the girls to understand that studying nonfiction causes us to revise ourselves as we gather, keep in our heads and hearts, and respond to new information. Indeed, once we've discovered and written about cicadas or Mars or the civil rights movement, we are no longer the same person.

At the beginning of the unit, Jacqueline and Laura identify for their students each of the objectives, which they plan to focus on in mini-lessons or conferences; these include finding verifiable information, collecting it in an organized way, reflecting on it to grow insights, and writing about it in interesting ways that demonstrate new learning.

For example, Laura is meeting with student pairs to talk about finding verifiable information. I sit with her when she confers with two students, Marjorie and Anna, who are planning to write about Jupiter and are reading several books about the planet together. The girls tell us that, because the books have conflicting information on Jupiter's distance from Earth, the girls feel the more recent book must be correct. Even though they may be wrong, Laura is proud of them because they are evaluating and critiquing information. It matters less to her that her students know the correct distance to Jupiter than that they know that readers and writers evaluate information based on careful reading, prior knowledge, and logic.

## FIGURE 5-1

### Genres of Nonfiction Writing

**Nonfiction writing based largely on personal experience**

- personal narrative
- memoir
- procedural or "how-to"
- letter
- personal essay

**Nonfiction writing based largely on research**

- feature article
- book review
- author profile
- sports writing
- report
- literary essay
- informational picture book

**Nonfiction writing that combines personal experience and research**

- literary essay
- some "how-to"
- sports writing
- editorial
- letter

# What to Teach: Reports, Feature Articles, and Editorials

When we teach nonfiction writing, it is important to consider the general qualities of good writing regardless of genre, as well as the features that are specific to each genre. (See Figure 4-5.) In Chapter 6 I focus on the general qualities of good writing and how they influence revision. So here I focus on the features of individual genres. When planning a unit of study, I suggest teaching genres on a continuum, starting with what I've found students consider least difficult—reports—to what they consider most difficult—editorials.

## REPORTS

Reports inform readers of information the writer has discovered. Writing them requires the ability to collect and sift information, organize it, present it clearly and precisely, come to a conclusion based on it, and critically assess the piece for gaps in logic or any missing information. And these skills transfer. Teaching students to write reports on topics of interest to them provides a solid foundation for writing more sophisticated kinds of pieces.

Specifically, it's important to teach students how to narrow topics so that they are manageable, how to conduct research on their topic, and how to edit and embed quotes to support details and inform the reader. Students also need to know that, although reports may appear objective, they usually have a subtle slant on the information. This slant comes from the writer's decision about what information to include and leave out. For example, a writer may aim to craft a neutral report on a controversial topic such as stem-cell research. But if she doesn't gather arguments from both sides, and present them in a balanced way, her piece will be slanted in one direction. On the other hand, some reports very clearly present one side at the expense of the other. The implication for teaching revision is that students must revise to balance information but also recognize that by processing information, they develop a slant toward it. Revision helps them recognize slant and keep it to a minimum.

## FEATURE ARTICLES

The next most sophisticated genre is the feature article. To write a good feature article, students must possess all the skills required to write a good report. However, feature articles differ from reports in that writers clearly make their slant known. Feature articles are frequently written in a conversational tone and contain revealing anecdotes and quotes that support the writer's position. Writers usually choose only information that makes their slant more compelling, although they may acknowledge that other ideas exist. As with report writers, their purpose is to inform, but their view on the topic is more obvious.

## EDITORIALS

To write an editorial, a writer needs to understand all aspects of a topic so well that he or she can convey a strong, convincing opinion about it. The opinion, rather than the information itself, is the focus of an editorial. In this genre, the writer is center stage, advocating a particular viewpoint based on selected pieces of information. Often the writer situates the information within a larger context to justify his point of view. Quotes and anecdotes may be used, but only to support or build sympathy for the writer's position. The writing is subjective. While the writer may acknowledge that other opinions exist, it is only to question and sometimes discredit them.

## WHY TEACHING THESE GENRES ON A CONTINUUM WORKS

- Students learn the basics of nonfiction writing through reports—finding a topic about which they care deeply, researching it, organizing information they find in their research, and presenting it to inform readers.

- When they write feature articles, students use information they find to arrive at new understandings about the topic. These new understandings often translate into a slant, and students write feature articles using facts to support the slant.

- The editorial is the most sophisticated genre of nonfiction because students must not only find and process facts, they must form a strong opinion based on them. Only from a thorough understanding of the facts can one have a valid, defendable opinion.

By teaching these genres successively, we can develop students' writing and thinking skills in nonfiction.

From there, Jacqueline and Laura ask students to use those thinking skills to decide what to write and how to write it. So Marjorie and Anna evaluate the facts they collect to decide which ones to include in their feature articles. Because Jacqueline and Laura have taught them that nonfiction writers have a responsibility to give their readers accurate, well-organized information, the girls take this step very seriously. They conclude that they must (*a*) check their facts against more than one source, (*b*) judge whether each fact is significant enough to include, and (*c*) be ready to change facts if new information is uncovered. All of this can be done before they begin composing; however, it should continue once they've begun their drafts to give them material for revision.

# HOW TO STUDY A NONFICTION MENTOR AUTHOR

Once you have introduced students to using mentor authors as a revision strategy for fiction writing, extend what they've learned to nonfiction texts.

One of the first points you should help them understand is that all nonfiction texts do not sound the same. A sports article, for example, sounds very different from a report, though the two pieces of writing may contain some of the same features, such as facts and quotes from experts. Sports articles often have short sentences, as if the writer is re-creating the quick movements of the game. Some nonfiction texts, such as *Night in the Country* by Cynthia Rylant, are poetic. Others, such as nonfiction books about science or social studies, often use compelling questions and shocking facts to interest readers. Each nonfiction genre has its own sound, and once students understand that concept and have read enough nonfiction to hear those sounds for themselves, they can begin to apply that understanding to their own writing.

Imagine snow falling silently in the great woodlands of North America. The only sounds are from the trees creaking and tossing in the wind. Suddenly the quiet is broken by the eerie howling of a wolf. And all the frightening stories and legends that you've heard about the treacherous and sly wolf and the evil werewolf begin to race through your mind.

But what is this animal of our imaginations truly like? Are wolves savage and destructive hunters of people and livestock? Or are they one of nature's most misunderstood creatures? It is possible that people don't like wolves because they don't know very much about them. For example, there is no record of a healthy wolf ever trying to kill a human in North America. Perhaps by learning about the wolf and how it lives in the natural world, we can begin to tell the difference between the real animal and the fables we've created.

**FIGURE 5-2**

*Page 1 of* Wolves *by Seymour Simon*

# Reading for Revision Strategies

Jacqueline decides to model revising nonfiction over several days using the first page of *Wolves* by Seymour Simon, because it is an effective example of fine nonfiction writing. She has read this book to the students before, so they are familiar with it. Her goal, of course, is to teach the class ways to revise its own work. (See Figure 5-3.)

FIGURE 5-3

## Revision Ideas Gleaned from the First Page of *Wolves* by Seymour Simon

| WHAT SEYMOUR SIMON DID | HOW I CAN REVISE MY WRITING |
|---|---|
| Text moves quickly to evoke fears and apprehension and to ask compelling questions | • Check the pace of my writing—don't let it lag<br>• Use readers' fears or worries as a hook<br>• Ask compelling questions to pull reader in |
| Every sentence does some work; there are no wasted words or descriptions | • Check for extra words, including phrases like *at this point in time* and *now*<br>• Check that no sentences repeat information or contain no information |
| The setting is exact and perfect details bring the reader to the place | • State the setting through precise details that make readers feel like they are there |
| Reader is addressed in the second person | • I can use the "you" voice to be more personal, but it will sound less formal |
| The author uses exciting verbs | • I can go through and change ordinary verbs |
| The author asks questions to reveal his slant | • Add in questions that I know the answer to but my reader doesn't know yet |
| The author suggests a change of attitude toward the subject—a "sales pitch"—if we keep on reading | • I can tell my reader the benefits of reading on<br>• I can make the reader think he may be wrong about my topic |
| A well-chosen fact supports the writer's slant | • Use really strong facts in places where they can help me make my point |
| There's a clear sentence that says what the writer is going to do in the book | • Somewhere at the beginning, I have to let my readers know what I'm going to write about |

Jacqueline shows students that by carefully looking at the writing work Simon has done, rather than getting caught up in the information itself, they can teach themselves to write compelling nonfiction, or at least to revise their nonfiction in successful ways.

## Raising the Level of Revision Work

Sometimes writers want to create a specific effect, such as build tension or create a context for nonfiction information. Often they will decide to define unusual words within the context in order to support reader understanding. Jacqueline decides that in order to move her students toward independence, she must teach them not only to identify revision strategies in mentor texts but also to search those texts deliberately for techniques they want to use. In other words, she wants to move her students from "Let me see all the things that Simon did" to "I want to create tension, so I'll study Simon to see how he did it." Encouraging students to think this way makes revision study more purposeful. They study mentor authors to find exactly what they want or need to learn. As such, teaching and learning become driven by student needs rather than by chance.

FIGURE 5-4

## Ways Nonfiction Writers Define Unfamiliar, Unusual, or Content-Related Words Within the Text

| WHAT SIMON DOES | EXAMPLE FROM *WOLVES* |
| --- | --- |
| Puts definitions of words inside parentheses | • . . . called *Canis lupus* (*canis* means dog and *lupus* means wolf)<br>• Hybrids (mixtures) such as wolf-dogs . . . |
| Uses parentheses to include synonyms or clarification | • These include tundra (or arctic) wolves . . . |
| Clarifies a word for readers by defining it at the end of a list | • . . . the coyote, the jackal, and a dog of Australia called the dingo. |
| Uses a word he's defined before and makes it part of the sentence, though he still gives readers clues about the meaning | • . . . the red wolf is really a hybrid, a mixture of wolf and coyote. |

**EXAMPLE #1:** Caroline is writing about snakes, and she must define lots of new words for her readers. Up to this point, Caroline has been defining words with declarative, dull sentences: "The meaning of the word *venom* means 'poison.'" So Jacqueline shows Caroline that she can search nonfiction texts to see how writers teach their readers new words. Now Caroline has several ways to embed definitions of new words in her text. (See Figure 5-4.)

**EXAMPLE #2:** Jacqueline has found that the writing of some students lacks energy, especially in the middle of their texts. These students can write interesting beginnings, but from there they lose momentum. So she calls these students together into a small group and shows them what Simon does in the middle of *Wolves*. From there, students use the information to create a plan for their own writing. (See Figure 5-5.)

This kind of thorough and careful study helps students become confident revisers. It gives them two ways to approach revision: as an inquiry into possibilities and as a search for answers to specific questions.

FIGURE 5-5

## Ways Nonfiction Writers Create Strong "Middles" to Sustain Reader Interest

| WHAT SIMON DOES | WHAT I CAN DO TO REVISE |
|---|---|
| Middle is just as interesting as beginning because he didn't tell everything up front, but chose to "string the reader along" | I must plan out where to include interesting facts rather than just plopping them in anywhere; I parcel them out carefully |
| The author organizes facts into important groups | I must know my topic well and know a lot about it in order to decide what to tell reader |
| The author probably had more information, but he decided to include only some of it | I will decide what to leave in or take out—what is interesting and what is important; I can use some information in a sidebar |
| The categories have a logic to their order, because the reader needs to digest information from one before she can understand the information in the next | I might have to shuffle my chunks of information so the arrangement makes better sense—this will help my reader to stay interested |
| The author provides facts, but also commentary | I must be sure to put in my thinking about the facts, because including only the facts can be boring |

# How to Teach Students to Collect a Variety of Mentor Texts to Fit Their Needs

Of course, only one mentor text can't provide all the answers to all revision questions for all genres. For example, as well written as *Wolves* is, it does not contain answers to genre-specific questions about sports writing. While good writing in any genre contains many of the same qualities, genre-specific qualities are best studied using writing in that genre. Therefore, we need to teach students to find mentor authors in many genres so that they have texts for many purposes. Students should have a variety of nonfiction texts available to them in the classroom library and/or writing center. Ideally students would find these texts on their own, but more likely you will need to do much of the legwork for them. You can begin by searching children's magazines such as the ones listed in the box on page 108 for editorials, feature articles, reports, and so on. I've found that tracking down high-quality essays for children is difficult, although I've had some luck online with www.teenink.com. If you're up to the challenge, you may want to write short pieces yourself for the class.

Once you have found good pieces in a cross section of genres, establish a filing system for them so students can easily locate them. If possible, laminate the pieces so they will last a long time, and keep a master photocopy in your own file.

Use the pieces in mini-lessons to demonstrate revision techniques the writers use, and then let students try those techniques as part of their independent work or as part of full-fledged unit of study on revision. (See Chapter 8.) It is important to remember that we want students to study and apply techniques on their own, so that eventually they can revise independently.

Students need to understand that when they are writing in a particular genre, they should have an exemplary piece of writing in that genre to study as a mentor text. (All students do not need the same text.) They should refer to the text as they compose and revise, because no matter how good their skills or intentions are, most likely their draft will need revision. Having a mentor text available makes it much easier for them to do that. As soon as they complete their first draft, they can look within their mentor text for revision ideas.

# How to Cover Revision, Day by Day, Within a Nonfiction Unit of Study

In a nonfiction unit of study, we teach students many skills about reading and writing nonfiction, including gathering and organizing information, providing details, and so on. After students have drafted, we teach them revision over a number of days. Here are several scenarios for how to organize those days. I also encourage you to search texts on your own and to read *Nonfiction Craft Lessons* by Ralph Fletcher and JoAnn Portalupi (Stenhouse, 2001) to expand your knowledge.

## Scenario 1: Revising Information

### DAY 1

**TEACHING POINT:** Writers decide which information is important and which is supporting detail. They use important information as organizational headings, and details to support this information. Notice how chapter headings and subheadings in our mentor texts provide important information.

**STUDENT WORK:** Reread your draft to be sure you have used important information as a way to organize your details.

### DAY 2

**TEACHING POINT:** Writers use quotes from reliable sources to support their points. Notice that in the mentor texts, writers tell us where they've gotten their information. They often tell us the credentials of a person they directly quote.

**STUDENT WORK:** Check that you've included information about sources to give weight to quotes, and make sure the sources are reliable.

### DAY 3

**TEACHING POINT:** Writers decide which information to include and which to leave out. Sometimes the length of the piece will determine this; sometimes the information itself is extraneous.

**STUDENT WORK:** Reread your draft and weigh each piece of information. Ask yourself if it really belongs in your writing, and if not, cross it out. Save it to use another time.

## Great Magazines for a Nonfiction Unit of Study

If you're looking for good examples of short nonfiction pieces to use as models in mini-lessons and conferences, check out these magazines:

- **Cobblestone publications (all at www.cobblestonepub.com):**
  *Appleseeds*       *Dig*
  *Ask*              *Faces*
  *Calliope*         *Footsteps*
  *Cobblestone*      *Muse*
  *Cricket*          *Odyssey*

- *National Geographic Explorer* (www.nationalgeographic.com)

- *New Moon* (www.newmoon.org)

- *Ranger Rick* (www.nationalwildlifefederation.org)

- **Scholastic publications (all at www.teacher.scholastic.com/ products/classmags.htm):**
  *DynaMath*
  *Scholastic News*
  *SuperScience*

- *Sports Illustrated for Kids* (www.sikids.com)

- *Time for Kids* (www.timeforkids.com)

### DAY 4

**TEACHING POINT:** Writers use different text features to communicate information. Notice how some mentor texts have charts and photos, some have bolded information, and some have sketches.

**STUDENT WORK:** Consider how you can include other text features to communicate information to your reader. Use your mentor author to help you make a decision.

## Scenario 2: Revising Genre

### DAY 1

**TEACHING POINT:** Writers make sure their writing has the features of the genre. Feature articles are different from reports, sports writing, editorials, and so on.

**STUDENT WORK:** Reread your mentor text. Use the sound of it to guide you as you reread your draft. Make changes in word choice, length of sentences, voice, use of anecdotes, and so on to fit the sound of your nonfiction genre.

### DAY 2

**TEACHING POINT:** Writers consider their audience as they write. Each mentor text we've read has an audience in mind.

**STUDENT WORK:** Think about your audience. If you could talk to them, how would you tell them your information? Reread your draft to match how you would talk to your audience with the writing you've done.

**TEACHING POINT:** Writers include different types of information, depending on genre. For example, Simon's *Wolves* has much more information than a poem on wolves might have.

**STUDENT WORK:** Reread your draft to see if the depth of your information fits with your genre. For example, a report will be more fact-filled than a feature article. Feature articles may have anecdotes, while reports usually don't.

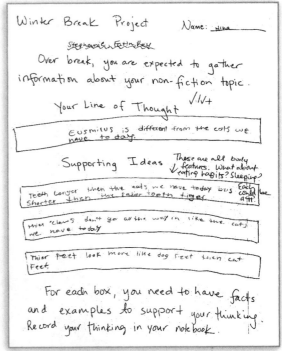

A fifth grader plans nonfiction writing by organizing and revising ideas before composing.

# SUMMARY

Students need to study mentor authors for nonfiction as much as for fiction. Nonfiction writing requires students to collect and categorize information, and process it to come to new understandings. Contrary to what many young writers think, writing good nonfiction requires as much craft as good fiction. Modeling revision using our own writing and using mentor authors provides students with concrete ways to write strong and successful reports, feature articles, editorials, and other nonfiction genres.

## Some Points to Remember

• Nonfiction writing must be as well crafted as fiction.

• There are many genres of nonfiction, and students should learn to write several of them.

• Students need lots of practice writing and revising nonfiction throughout the year and across the content areas.

• Nonfiction mentor author studies help students see how they can improve their writing and become independent revisers of nonfiction.

# CHAPTER SIX

# REVISING ACCORDING TO THE QUALITIES OF GOOD WRITING

When I taught fourth grade in the Bronx, my classroom was on the fifth floor of a sturdy brick building built in the 1920s. The stairwells were thick with decades of gray paint and the odor of liberally applied disinfectant, and the doors, windows, and floor in my classroom were old and worn. Every morning I opened the door to decades of chalk and ink and paper and the smell of old varnish on the heavy wood trim and old paint on the walls. It smelled the same—day in and day out—as it had years earlier, when I was a child walking those halls.

I think back on my early teaching and realize how, in some ways, it was not so different from the teaching I received as a child. Like so many teachers, I taught the way I had been taught. I called students up to my desk—Jason, Anthony, Frances—and told them how to "improve" their writing. I looked at writing from a deficit perspective—what is "wrong" that needs to be "fixed." The problem was that I didn't know much about revision at the time; I didn't know that revision provided an opportunity to clarify one's thinking. I knew only what I had been taught by my teachers, and that wasn't much. So I said things to my students like, "Go fix your beginning" and "Write a better ending" and "Correct your spelling." I confess there were even times I told them the exact words to write. My teaching was hollow. I was not showing those children how to fix beginnings, write better endings, or correct their spelling. So when they went back to their desks and sat there in frustration, it was my fault. I didn't know what else to say to them. I didn't know enough about revision or the qualities of good writing. Furthermore, I didn't yet understand that giving students choices in writing leads them to independence.

Studying good writing and the qualities of good writing—focus, word choice, elaboration, organization, fluency, conventions, voice, sense of audience, and genre—would have made all the difference to my teaching in those days. It would have given structure and meaning to my revision suggestions, and it would have made my students understand the reasons behind revision.

Keeping qualities of good writing in mind while teaching revision makes instruction less random and more focused. Often students choose revision strategies from a class chart with no *reason* for doing so. They merely sprinkle on revisions as though they're seasoning soup. In order to give meaning to revisions, we should teach them what the qualities of good writing are, and then teach them revision strategies that will help them apply each quality in their own writing. In this chapter, I look at the following:

- the qualities of good writing and what they mean

- revision strategies for each quality

- ways to help students be deliberate in their strategy choices

# The Qualities of Good Writing and What They Mean

"The qualities of good writing." It's a phrase we hear quite often in education today, especially in connection with state and local writing tests. Regardless of how you feel about writing tests, these qualities do define elements of good writing. They give us a standard for assessing student writing and for planning our teaching. They give us a common language about writing. In many ways, they clarify and simplify our work.

Being able to identify, explain, and apply each quality is crucial to producing excellent writing consistently. Instruction in one or more of these qualities should be included in every unit of study you plan, regardless of its genre focus or topic, through whole-group, small-group, or individual instruction.

There are several outstanding instructional models that isolate qualities of good writing, including the widely used 6+1 Traits model developed by the Northwest Regional Educational Laboratory in the mid-1980s (Culham, 2003; Spandel, 2001), which advocates assessing student writing for ideas, organization, voice, word choice, sentence fluency, conventions, and presentation to plan instruction. If you want more information on the traits of writing, consult the definitive resource, *6+1 Traits of Writing: The Complete Guide, Grades 3 and Up*, by Ruth Culham (Scholastic, 2003).

Another model is Carl Anderson's, which encourages us to focus on meaning, genre, structure, detail, voice, and conventions (in press). Anderson arrived at these qualities after conferring with hundreds of students. JoAnn Portalupi and Ralph Fletcher (2004) urge us to base our instruction on ideas, design, language, and presentation.

Each of these models is unique and outstanding in its own way, and I advise you to study them and use what's most useful to plan instruction. In the discussion that follows, I explore qualities from each of these models—and include a couple of my own, based on what I see in classrooms on a regular basis.

## Focus

Focus is the main idea—the heart of the topic that the writer explores and stays within. It should be significant yet limited in scope. Donald Murray (1985) calls it "that point at which writers concentrate their attention." The topic should be significant or meaningful to the writer, or made significant or meaningful by the writer. Lucy Calkins (1994) teaches us that significance is found by the writer through the process of writing. The skillful writer can take a topic that appears unimportant and make it fascinating.

Murray goes to say, "The primary focusing technique is the focusing line to capture the starting point of the drafting process." A good focusing line captures a tension, conflict, problem, irony, or contradiction in the subject; it gives the writer energy to pursue potential meaning. The topic is clear and the writer's angle on the topic is also clear. For young writers, this means stating in two or three sentences what the piece is about, then remaining true to that topic in the writing, or skillfully winding back to it after weaving in an anecdote or purposeful digression.

Focus also requires the writer to narrow his or her topic. Donald Murray (1985) says that the way to write about something big is to write small about it— for example, to write about the horrors of war, you might write about a child's bloody sock. In fact, he says writers usually work from the specific to the general, and that while they "value accurate, specific information as supporting evidence . . . they also see detail as inspiring meaning." Eudora Welty (1984) says, "What discoveries I've made in the course of writing stories all begin with the particular, never the general." Students must learn that good writers often tell only a part of the story. So, part of teaching students to focus their work is to work on narrowing their scope.

## Word Choice

When writers use precise words, they exhibit an appreciation for the beauty of language and for the power of words to express shades of meaning. Toni Cade Bambara (1980) tells us, "Words are to be taken seriously. I try to take seriously acts of language. Words set things in motion. I've seen them doing it. Words conjure. I try not to be careless about what I utter, write, sing. I'm careful about what I give voice to."

Include time for "word work" in your writing workshop, time for discussing and collecting words (Heard, 2003) and for developing a fascination with them (Allen, 1999; Beck, McKeown, & Kucan, 2002; Greenwood, 2004). Model searching for the perfect word in your own writing, and collect exciting words from your reading to use in later writing. Be sure to use and repeat a wide range of interesting words when you speak—mention how ominous the sky looks or how apprehensive you feel. Model playing with language to find exact words—"Today's weather is lovely. No, scrumptious. No, exquisite. No, celestial." You will notice students beginning to use these words in their speaking and writing before long. Mem Fox (1992) says, "The choice of words is as crucial as the choice of notes in a fugue."

Students must learn that good writers must choose words carefully. They also omit and delete words that are not critical to understanding the story.

## Elaboration

Elaboration means using examples, explanation, and description to extend the topic. The writer may stretch out a thought, add details, and/or editorialize. Elaboration is important because it demonstrates the writer's depth of knowledge, as well as his or her willingness to aid the reader in understanding the piece.

In an effort to teach students to elaborate, sometimes we unwittingly teach them to "overwrite" or pad their writing by saying something again and again. Teaching students to write two pages when only a half page is needed is not good teaching. William Zinsser (1994) writes, "Clutter is the disease of American writing. We are a society strangling in unnecessary words, circular constructions, pompous frills and meaningless jargon." Teach students to elaborate only when it's appropriate, only when they have a point that is important enough for them to elaborate on. In that case, teach them to elaborate by stretching their thinking to say more, not merely by finding synonyms or saying the same thing many different ways.

## Organization

The writer has a plan or logical framework for how the writing will unfold. This framework is clear to the writer and the reader, and is deliberately chosen to convey meaning. It fits the purpose and/or genre of the particular piece. Organization is important because it shows the writer's ability to present ideas in a way that the reader will comprehend, as well as his or her ability to categorize and create order.

## Fluency

When writers have mastered fluency, their writing flows from sentence to sentence, paragraph to paragraph, and section to section effectively and effortlessly. Sentences are beautifully constructed and varied in length. They are direct, easy to read, and contain no muddy images or confusing tangents. Transitions are smooth. Fluent writing demonstrates that the writer has an ear for the rhythm, cadence, and conventions of spoken language. As a result, the reader is more able to follow the writer's thinking.

## Conventions

The writer uses grammar and punctuation not only correctly but deliberately and thoughtfully to convey meaning, which means bending the rules occasionally. Katie Ray (1999) writes at length about using grammar and punctuation to shape thought. Young writers who believe that conventions are nothing but rules to obey are missing out on a great revision tool (Angelillo, 2002). If we want students to use complicated sentence structures in their writing, C. A. Daiute (1982) advises us to have students study models of sentences with such structures, rather than having them diagram sentences or correct incorrect sentences in exercises (see Chapter 9). Constance Weaver (1996) tells us that grammar is not a series of disembodied rules but a system for how language works. Writers who use conventions successfully demonstrate respect for their writing and for their readers.

## Voice

Voice is the writer's personality coming through the words. Tom Romano (2004) calls voice the "presence" of the writer and passionately advocates for bold writing with "the sound of your voice in [your reader's] head."

Often teachers wonder how to teach voice to students. Lee Edgerton (2003) advises us that voice depends on tone, rhythm, vocabulary, and imagery. When we read Anna Quindlen or Sharon Creech, we "hear" their voices talking directly to us, and if we look carefully at their writing, we see they use precise words to indicate tone, they use punctuation to re-create how the sentences should be read, and they create images in our minds through analogies, asides, and commentary. When we teach voice, we show students these ways to re-create their spoken voices in writing.

# The Qualities of Good Teaching

Many of the qualities of good writing can be applied to good teaching. They provide a strong framework for measuring the effectiveness of our teaching and our chances for success.

## FOCUS

Good teaching must have a focus each day and across the year. When planning lessons, ask yourself, "What is the one thing I want to teach, and what do I expect students will be able to do at the end?" Tell students *exactly* what you are teaching them and *exactly* how the example you are using demonstrates what you are teaching. Also be very specific about what you want students to do when they are writing; tell them what their writing work for the day is. Write it on a chart, overhead transparency, or smart board.

Be sure that each lesson is based on something meaningful and significant to students. Be sure your teaching is clear and simple. Decide the best way to make your teaching point. Is it to model from your own writing? To use a mentor text or short shared text? To act out a conversation with a student or another teacher? *How* you teach is just as important as *what* you teach.

## WORD CHOICE

Choose your words carefully, not only to make your teaching clear but also to show your love of language. Your students will come to love words if you love them, if you savor and respect them, and if you use them to convey your passion, knowledge, and thinking.

## ELABORATION

Use one *perfect* example of what you are teaching, rather than four not-so-perfect ones. Do not elaborate by reteaching yesterday's lesson, but by expanding on points or principles that students aren't grasping or they find particularly interesting. If students need a refresher, tell them what you want them to recall, and move quickly into the day's lesson.

## ORGANIZATION

Organize your year according to units of study, and organize your lessons within each unit of study. Be sure your lessons follow a careful sequence so that students see your line of thinking from day to day. Choose text samples and make transparencies and charts ahead of time. Gather supplies such as books and markers in the meeting area so you won't need to fuss around looking them in the middle of a lesson. Finally, organize the room, the physical space, in a way that maximizes every inch.

## FLUENCY

Lessons that flow from one logical topic to the next support student learning because you're not always shifting in different directions. Remember that you cannot teach students everything there is to know; teach a few things deeply and well, in a sequence that makes sense. In addition, each lesson should follow a predictable pattern: connect your lesson topic to the previous topics, teach by modeling or demonstrating, give students a chance to try out what you're teaching, and send them off with a work plan for that day.

## SENSE OF AUDIENCE

Obviously, you must know your students well to teach them well. Assess students continuously throughout the year by observing them, conferring with them, and analyzing their work. Plan your lessons to fit your audience and its needs. Consider any special-needs students ahead of time and be sure to provide for them.

## Sense of Audience

The writer knows for whom he is writing, either explicitly or implicitly, and it comes through in the writing. Having a sense of audience is important because it drives the writer to speak to the specific needs of the reader. Even Mem Fox (1992) says, "[in] the 27 journals I have now filled . . . are examples of the sort of drivel people write when they know the audience isn't important." All too often, though, our students' only audiences are either the teacher or themselves. So it's important to give them a variety of authentic tasks designed for different end users.

## Genre

Most printed texts fit into certain categories—feature article, essay, story, poem, self-help, and so on. The writer creates expectations for the reader by labeling his or her writing a particular genre. As a reader, I expect to find certain elements in a mystery and others in a movie review. While it is true that some writing crosses genres—a nonfiction poem, or an essay that is also a review—most writing stays within the constraints of the genre in which it is written. For students, this means not drifting—for example, eliminating story when writing a science report, unless he or she is using anecdote by design. It also means we don't want "genre-less" writing—those pallid writing assignments we used to call "compositions," which are unlike any genre in the real world. Students should be able to name the genre they are writing, some of the features of the genre, and how their writing fits into it.

# REVISION STRATEGIES FOR EACH QUALITY

It is not effective to tell students to revise without teaching them exactly *how* to do it. In fact, the "how" should drive all our instruction. With that in mind, let's look at some ways to teach qualities of good writing.

## Teaching Focus

In order to teach students focus, we must show them that most writing has a "focusing line," as Donald Murray calls it, or a "topic sentence" that defines what the piece is about. In some pieces, this focusing line will be the first line in the piece, but this is neither necessary nor appropriate for all genres. Nevertheless, having a focusing line helps the reader and the writer know what to expect. With students whose writing wanders or is unclear, I suggest asking them to define their piece in one sentence and to write that sentence at the top of a notebook page. Students can work to revise that line for clarity and then return to their drafts to revise, using the focusing line as a barometer for all the writing.

We can use focus to show students to write specifically and with purpose. Some forms of writing, like personal narratives, work best if they focus on a specific event at a specific time, or a string of events that are related. When students are planning their writing, encourage them to narrow the scope. Thus, "my day at the amusement park" might become "the hot-dog-eating contest I had with my cousin before we both got sick on the roller coaster," or whatever moment the student chooses. For some students, this will be difficult. You may need to teach this strategy repeatedly, while they are planning and revising their writing. These lesson ideas will help:

Eva

I used to live in an apartment and I shared a bedroom with my bratty older sister. But now my family just moved into a condo and I have my own bedroom. I love my bedroom and I don't have to tell my sister to shut up or to keep her stuff off my bed. Our new place even has a pool down the road and I am making lots of new friends. I have fun unpacking my boxes and finding new places to put all my things.

Things to work on:
1. Focus – what is the point of the story?

My family just moved from a crowded apartment to a big condo and I love our new place! I even have my very own bedroom and no longer have to share a bedroom with my bratty older sister or tell her to shut up and keep her stuff off my bed. The best part is there is a pool down the street and I can go swimming every day after school. I really like unpacking my boxes and finding places for all my things. I hope we never move again.

A fifth-grade student works on focus.

- Writers often make pictures in their minds to capture what they want to say accurately and clearly. Recall an event. Draw a sketch of the whole event; now choose one small part of the sketch and "blow it up" (Lane, 1993) by sketching that one part. What do you see? Write it.

- Writers try to retell an event the best way they can. Make a movie in your mind of the event. Say out loud what is happening, what it looks like, who is talking, and what they are saying. Then replay the movie in slow motion as you write it down, or ask a partner to take notes for you as you say it.

- Writers try to include their thinking in a personal narrative. Think of something that happened to you during the event. What was going through your mind? Try to reimagine one thing (Lane, 1993) and add it to your draft.

- Sometimes we say, "I was scared" or "I was excited." That doesn't tell your reader enough. Think about how it feels in your body when you are scared or excited. Describe that physical feeling, rather than telling us what it was—for example, "My heart was pounding and my mouth went dry."

- Writers have a reason for writing whatever they write. Sometimes it is to entertain, sometimes to inform, sometimes to warn. What is the purpose of your story? If it is to entertain, then your story must be interesting. Read your story aloud to a partner. Ask her to indicate places that are not interesting by raising her thumb as you read. Then go back to your notebook and revise those parts, or remove them if you don't need them. If you decide to remove them, make sure what's left makes sense. If it doesn't make sense, add, remove, or reorganize words until it does.

  If your purpose is to warn us—for example, "Don't eat a hot dog before you go on the roller coaster"—then everything in your story should fuel the situation that you're warning us about. Go back and remove anything that doesn't add to the situation. For example, details about the weather or crowds are only important if they added to your feeling of nausea.

  Once you know what your purpose is, you can measure everything you wrote against that purpose. As you reread each line of your draft, ask yourself, "Will this part help my readers understand what happened? Will it help them understand my purpose?" Go through and highlight/box out/underline anything that you are not sure about. Then work with a partner to decide whether to revise those parts or remove them.

## Teaching Elaboration

Elaborating can be a quick way to make writing better. Even students who are not fluent writers can feel a sense of accomplishment when they can choose from a menu of elaboration techniques and see their writing improve immediately. For example, rereading the entire piece will help students decide which parts to elaborate. Otherwise they will elaborate on all parts or on random parts, and that doesn't make for good writing—it makes for clutter. You can find useful techniques for craft in Katie Wood Ray's book *Wondrous Words* (NCTE, 1999) and in Ralph Fletcher and JoAnn Portalupi's *Craft Lessons* (Stenhouse, 1998).

Model elaborating for students on an overhead transparency using your own writing. Show them that elaboration means forcing yourself to think harder about

> Alison
>
> Last summer I went to camp for the first time. There were a lot of activities to do every day that made me tired. Every day I would go to different classes like pottery and arts and crafts. I liked the outdoor classes the best. *My counselor was really cool. Her name was Jen. She even let me sleep in the bunk bed next to my best friend Shari. I hope I get to go back to camp again this summer and I hope Jen is there too.
>
> There were a lot of outdoor activities like boating, hiking, fishing, and swimming that made me tired by the end of the day.
>
> My favorite class was arts and crafts where we learned how to make pottery and sew pillows.

*A student works on elaboration.*

## How Writers Elaborate

FIGURE 6-1

- Decrease the pace and write the event in slow motion
- Give supporting examples in groups of three
- Tell the internal story—what the character is thinking and feeling
- Add dialogue or a counterargument.
- Add examples from life
- Make connections to life, self, and other texts
- Paint a picture of the scene
- Write small lists about a topic or a phrase, then add items from the list to a sentence
- Add background information (what already happened or what's behind the action)
- Use flashback to fill in information
- Move from big broad statements to small ones

something in order to say more about it. Helpful ideas include visualizing how something looks or sounds, thinking about details or descriptive words, or adding in what a character says, does, or thinks. You can also point students to mentor authors to study how they elaborate. In the last chapter, we looked at some of Cynthia Rylant's work in *Night in the Country*. Notice how she uses appositives to add and clarify information, personification and onomatopoeia to add to setting, and a pattern of three examples to elaborate her ideas. Teach students to do this, as well as how to study other writers to discover how they elaborate on their ideas.

When teaching any quality of good writing, it's important to name how an author achieves the quality, rather than merely pointing out the quality and expecting students to apply it. In all our teaching, it is vital to tell students *what* we want them to do, tell them *why* we want them to do it, and show them *how* to do it.

## Teaching Organization

Planning the organization of a piece requires a large vision. However, most students work at the "word level"—that is, they think about a word, or maybe a sentence, and write it. We need to teach them how to step back and think about the bigger picture.

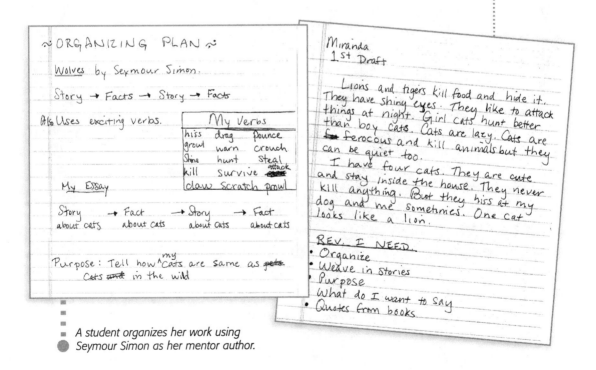

A student organizes her work using Seymour Simon as her mentor author.

of words on the page, revision becomes difficult. It often requires completely rethinking the writing, and lots of tedious recopying. To avoid this, have students study mentor texts to find simple, straightforward ways to organize their drafts, and teach them to think about organization while they are planning and, of course, when revising.

Two simple, straightforward organizational structures are the list and the story. A story contains a plot, or problem and solution with rising and falling action, whereas a list is a string of events with no tension driving them forward. I've found that students can easily grasp these structures and move onto more sophisticated ones from there, such as flashback, parallel plot structure, and multiple points of view. (See Figures 6-2 and 6-3.)

Also, teach students some of the "refinements" of organization, such as chunking information into paragraphs, using subheadings in nonfiction, and thinking in clear sections of beginnings, middles, and ends.

## Ways to Organize Lists and Model Texts

FIGURE 6-2

| WAYS TO ORGANIZE LISTS | TEXTS THAT DEMONSTRATE THE STRUCTURE |
| --- | --- |
| Make a big statement, followed by several long and detailed examples | *My Grandmother's Clock* by Geraldine McCaughrean |
| Make a big statement, followed by a short line of support, with a repeating refrain for emphasis | *Tough Boris* by Mem Fox |
| Use time to organize the list—for example hours, days, months, seasons, years | *My Mama Had a Dancing Heart* by Libba Moore Gray |
| Use superlatives to organize the list—for example, big, bigger, biggest | *Night Noises* by Mem Fox |

## Ways to Organize Stories and Model Texts

FIGURE 6-3

| WAYS TO ORGANIZE STORIES | TEXTS THAT DEMONSTRATE THE STRUCTURE |
| --- | --- |
| Start with the problem | *Smoky Night* by Eve Bunting |
| Start with everyday overview, then zoom in on one day when something special happened | *Miz Berlin Walks* by Jane Yolen *Dear Willie Rudd* by Libba Moore Gray |
| State what's happening now, then flash back to story | *White Socks Only* by Evelyn Coleman |
| Build through time to a crisis | *A Day's Work* by Eve Bunting |

# Teaching Fluency

I believe this quality may be difficult for some students because it almost requires having a musical ear, or at least being able to hear the cadences of language. Alice S. Horning (2004) calls this "meta-linguistic awareness." Read aloud slowly and thoughtfully, with attention to how sentences flow together smoothly. Let students hear the melodic quality of good writing, including transitions that cue readers to expect change. Students should hear that sentences are fluid until writers break the flow for effect. For example, in Karen Hesse's picture book *Come On, Rain!*, the sentences in the first half of the book are long and winding, with so many words and so much alliteration that readers feel the heaviness of the oppressive heat. But when the rain comes, Hesse changes the gears. She signals the change by using six single-syllable words—"and just like that rain comes"—mimicking the sounds of the first rain drops plopping on the sidewalk. Here are lessons you might teach for fluency:

- Writers make sure each part of their writing flows into the next part. This enables the reader to follow where the writer is going. Reread your draft to make sure your reader can follow your thinking.

- One way to help readers follow your writing is to use transition words and phrases. These words and phrases get readers from one part of the piece to the next and make the whole piece read smoothly. Some transition words and phrases move time—for example, "an hour later" lets the reader know that 60 minutes have passed. Others are "the next morning," "after breakfast," "soon," "in July," and so on. Look through your mentor texts and find transition words and phrases that move time. Then use some of them in your draft to move time along for your reader.

- Some transition phrases move the story from one part to the next by charting a character's actions—for example, "once she had packed her bag" or "before he could ride his bike." Look in your mentor texts again for transition phrases that move the story along; then use similar phrases in your draft to explain your character's actions and keep the story moving.

- The rhythm of sentences also makes writing fluid. Most writers try to vary the lengths of their sentences—some are long and some are short, and some are even fragments used for effect. For example, "I turned the corner, lost in the music from my Walkman, and nearly fell over a pile of junk on the sidewalk. It stopped me cold. Cold dead." Look in mentor texts to find passages containing sentences of various lengths, and think about the effect the variation creates. Then revise at least one place in your draft by varying the lengths of your sentences.

## Naming What We Notice in Writing

Isoke Nia, one of my mentors at the Teachers College Reading and Writing Project, says that it is not enough for students to notice what writers have done. They have to be able to "name" what writers have done. What she means is that students must be able to give names to strategies. Katie Wood Ray talks about this in her book *Wondrous Words* (1999). She says, "Names make it easier for individual writers to access crafting techniques in their thinking as they write. In a way, the names act as labels for what's in a writer's head about craft." Peter H. Johnston (2004) says that "noticing and naming things is a central part of [a writer's] apprenticeship."

For example, I would not teach students that Cynthia Rylant uses three words with the "o" sound in *Night in the Country*, because, while it is interesting to notice what she does, it won't help students in the long run. But naming the technique—"writers think about the sounds of vowels in the middle of words and sometimes repeat them"—gives students a way to use it in their own writing. By moving from noticing to naming, students can reproduce the technique.

## Teaching Conventions

I suggest scheduling a unit of study in conventions in the fall. During the unit, students study texts to see how writers use conventions. Students must understand that they can use conventions as a revision strategy to shape meaning. See Chapter 9 for more details. You can read more about studying conventions in my book *A Fresh Approach to Teaching Punctuation* (Scholastic, 2002).

## Teaching Voice

When writers write with voice, it sounds as if they are talking directly to their audience. Writers achieve voice by

- varying sentence structure and length
- using fragments deliberately
- choosing words that reveal emotion, attitude, character, culture, social status, and stance
- repeating phrases
- using colloquialisms, slang, or references to popular culture
- using conventions creatively
- recounting anecdotes
- addressing the audience directly to create a sense of intimacy
- including commentary
- using exaggeration or hyperbole
- using irony or sarcasm
- using figurative language
- applying an organization that leads readers along
- asking rhetorical questions

## Planning: The Key to Less Revising

Sometimes the amount of revision a writer needs to do depends on the amount of planning he or she has done. More planning before drafting means less revising after it gets going. Often the revision strategies we teach become internalized as planning strategies, such as organizing before drafting, using conventions to compose, and writing with elaboration; students begin to make many decisions like these before drafting.

However, too much planning can take the energy out of a draft and steal its freshness. As students begin to incorporate simple revision strategies into their original drafts, they'll need deeper and more sophisticated ways to revise. We don't want students to think that with lots of planning they can avoid revising entirely.

- use of punctuation to help the reader re-create the rhythm of spoken language, insert commentary, or pick up or slow down the pace

Use ideas from this list to teach students to revise lifeless writing so their voices come through.

Ruth Culham (2003) tells us that voice happens when the writer cares about the message. She says it is "the heart and soul of the writing, the magic, the wit, the feeling, the life and breath." Yet so often we ask students to write "objectively." Study texts with your class and you will see that the ones that you enjoy reading, regardless of genre or topic, are those filled with voice. Remember that even "academic" writing is fascinating when filled with detail, imagery, and tone because readers can connect to the information (Dean, 2000).

## Teaching a Sense of Audience

As I've stated earlier, many students believe the only audience for their writing is their teacher. This robs them of a powerful part of writing, the chance to communicate their thinking to others. We can teach students a sense of audience by using mentor texts to imagine for whom the writer wrote each one. For example, some picture books are written for very young children, and students can see that in the word choice and layout of the books. On the other hand, sports magazines are written for sports enthusiasts, which we can see from the writers' word choices and their assumption of background knowledge. By showing students a variety of texts, you can make them aware of how writers have a sense of who their audience is.

- Ask students to name the exact audience for whom they are writing: other students in the class, the fourth graders down the hall, prospective readers of a new book, their grandparents, and so on.

- Ask them to think about how their writing fits that audience in terms of the words they use, their topic choice, their stance on the topic, the voice, and the amount of factual evidence they include.

- Help students find mentor texts that match their intended audience. Study them together to see what the writer did; name specific features and use them in revision.

- Test the writing out with the intended audience, if possible. See how the audience responds and ask for recommendations for change.

## Teaching Genre

Many of your units of study will be organized around studying genres. You can use the charts you've made for each genre as guidelines for students to follow as they write. Of course, mentor texts in the genre are essential, because students can compare their writing to the mentor text and determine how well their writing fits the genre.

Some students want to write in only one genre, usually one in which they feel comfortable. In order to provide them with the best writing experience, I suggest you coach them to write in other genres, and then let them choose their favorite as an independent writing project. They may also try revising their favorite genre to fit into other genres. For example, a student who writes a personal narrative about a roller-coaster ride might be persuaded to write a report on roller coasters. It is most important that students name their genre and how their writing fits into it.

# Summary

As we teach revision, we keep in mind qualities of good writing to teach in every unit of study. This framework will keep our instruction from becoming scattered or random, because we'll be grounded by these big qualities we know students must learn. Be less concerned with how each student's writing looks than with how each student is growing and taking risks as a writer. Even if a student hasn't grown as much as you'd like, have faith that as the year progresses, all the demonstration, practice, and feedback that you're giving students will pay off. If you base your instruction in developing qualities of good writing, your students will grow as writers.

## Some Points to Remember

- You can't teach all revision strategies in one unit of study.

- It's not enough to tell students what to do; you have to tell them how to do it.

- In every unit of study, you want students to feel successful revising, but you'll begin to layer on more complex strategies.

- The qualities of good writing provide a bank from which to draw many ideas for revision lessons.

# CHAPTER SEVEN

# DEEPENING THE STUDY OF REVISION ACROSS THE YEAR

**W**hen I was taking sailing lessons, my very wise teacher, Gordon, knew just how much work to give me each time we met. He knew he had to keep me interested in the work but not make the tasks so monumental that I would throw up my hands in frustration and walk away. So for each lesson he taught me some small task at which I could feel successful. At first I was not ready to handle the main mast or heavy wind or racing, but he knew I'd get there eventually if he could just keep me going. Eventually I'd be ready for nuanced and deeper study; eventually I'd have the confidence and courage to do more.

Teaching revision works the same way. You must start students with simple strategies with which they can feel instant success and then fold in deeper, more intensive strategies as the year goes on. You must get them to feel successful and then extend the strategies you've taught them.

One way to do this is to consider which revision strategies lend themselves to the topic of each unit of study you plan. For example, organization and voice lend themselves perfectly to a unit of study on report writing. Reports must be well organized to be clear and keep the reader's interest, and contrary to students' perceptions of them, the best ones are full of voice. While you might teach these qualities of good writing before students start drafting, take them on again as they revise. Obviously, you'll teach all qualities of good writing all year long, but it's effective and efficient to emphasize certain ones, depending on genre. If you fold qualities into every unit of study strategically, your writing workshop will support revision all year and prepare students for deep revision.

The writer who is ready for deep revision is able to do all the simple revision strategies I've mentioned, and choose them appropriately to meet their purposes for writing. He may have made his writing better, but he wants to do more. He identifies points where his reader may be confused or where the writing is awkward or dull. By recognizing these problems with his writing, this student has reached a milestone. He knows he needs to cast his net wider for revision techniques. Murray (1999) suggests that we ask two questions as revisers: "What works?" and "What needs

## Reading for Targeted Revision

It is almost impossible to read a draft and revise for everything. Usually, there is just too much for the writer to do. One solution is to teach students to read their drafts several times, choosing *one* revision point each time. Writers often develop a "system" for rereading—that is, they may read for meaning first and reread for word choice last. No one way is best. So ask students to decide for themselves how they will reread to revise. To help them, you might write on a chart a menu of possibilities for ways to reread, like the one below. I prefer giving students choice, especially after they've gained experience revising.

- Reread to make sure that you've said what you meant to say.

- Reread looking for holes or missing information.

- Reread for the sense of how each section flows into the next.

- Reread for consistent tone.

- Reread for logical order.

- Reread for sentence flow.

- Reread for word choice.

- Reread to balance any two components (for example, dialogue and narration, fact and opinion, and so on).

- Reread for the strength of each section (for example, solid ending, energetic middle, and so on).

work?" The student who is ready for deep revision asks both questions even after a first revision is done.

In the early-in-the-year units we coach students to accept revising as part of a writer's process. In subsequent units we keep this energy alive by teaching them additional strategies, increasing their knowledge of mentor authors, and nudging them toward independence. In this chapter I look at extending students' repertoire of revision strategies throughout the year. Specifically, I show you how to

- plan a second unit of study
- plan revision for the remainder of the year
- teach additional deep revision strategies for any time of year

# PLANNING A SECOND UNIT OF STUDY

After you've carried out the first unit of study, in which you have established a safe learning community and taught students how to keep a notebook and go through the writing process, it is time to move to another unit in which students put everything they've learned into action. Many teachers choose to focus their second unit on personal narrative, because students' experiences give them so much to write about. Lucy Calkins recommends focusing on personal narrative in a second unit, and suggests we do it in October. She feels there is so much to teach that strengthens students' writing muscles for the year ahead, such as writing a story with a clear ending, maintaining a consistent point of view, and focusing on one event.

On the other hand, some teachers do a different unit of study, due to the timing of state tests or their district's requirements. They may focus on teaching students to narrow their focus, or choose an organizing structure for their writing, and to begin to pay careful attention to word choice, because these skills will improve their writing dramatically and quickly. In some cases, teachers may decide to teach

## Other Possible Genres to Teach as Units of Study

- memoir
- realistic fiction
- poetry
- feature article
- report
- essay
- book review

nonfiction writing at this time in preparation for grade-level requirements through-out the year.

Everything you do in your classroom should be based on your ongoing assessment of what your students need. (See Chapters 2 and 10 for ways to assess.) Let's assume for a moment that you've taught two or three strategies for elaboration in the personal narrative unit of study. Again, based on your students' needs and their writing experience and grade level, you will want to include revision strategies for other qualities of good writing. Remember that when we have a vision of what we want to teach about revision across the school year, we'll add to the students' bank of revision strategies little by little. Therefore, when planning your second unit of study, consider not only genre but also revision skills students need to develop early in order to practice them all year.

## Revising Personal Narratives

Since personal narrative is so popular as a second unit of study among teachers, I'm going to use it as an example to show how to plan, carry out, and teach revision strategies. Personal narratives work best if students focus on a specific event at a specific time, such as moving to a new home, or a string of related events, such as spending every summer at grandmother's house. When students are planning their narratives, encourage them to narrow the scope, because narratives that tell the entirety of an event can become long and unwieldy. Also, it is much easier for students to write well about a narrowly focused story or a short period of time: "the argument I had with my brother waiting on line for the scariest roller coaster" usually works better than "my trip to the theme park." Ralph Fletcher (1993) advises us, "The bigger the issue,

### What Is a Personal Narrative Unit of Study?

Personal narrative is a story from one's own life. By teaching it, we show students that writers get ideas from their lives, and that the smallest moments in life contain stories if we know how to find them. In a personal narrative unit of study, students often write about something that happened to them, often something quite ordinary. Their main goal should be drawing readers into the moment, rather than accurately relating the story. Teaching focuses on helping students apply the writing-process stages they learned in the first unit, and on how to tell a story by zooming in on a small event, creating significance from the event, writing dialogue, and evoking time and place. After students have drafted, teaching turns toward revision, often focusing on qualities of good writing.

the smaller you write" and "The writing becomes beautiful when it becomes specific." This focusing of a personal narrative topic can happen while students are planning and revising their writing. In this section, I suggest ways to help students once they have those initial ideas down. I concentrate on revising at the word level, the sentence level, and the "chunk" level.

## Revising at the Word Level

Words are all a professional writer has to express the condition of her heart, the thoughts in her mind, the feelings in her soul. Writers love words—they love the way words sound, they love rolling words around in their mouths, collecting them, discovering new ones, making lists, and playing with them. Writers also use literary devices such as onomatopoeia and assonance. We can teach students to love words and use devices the same way professional writers do. Here's how.

Talk about words every day in the classroom. Teach students that curiosity about words and what they mean and how they sound is part of a writer's life; in fact, developing a sense of language—words, grammatical structures—is important not only as a "mode of inquiry, but also as an object worthy of inquiry" (Lee, 2000). Show students how much you love words: the way they sound, the subtle differences in their meanings, the music they create when they're put together in a certain way. Give students opportunities to talk about words *as they find them in reading*, rather than copying them down to look up later. Wonder aloud why an author chose a word in a particular context, how certain words have multiple meanings, and how context clues you in to meanings. This type of work is a foundation for all formal vocabulary instruction, which we also must include in our instruction (Allen, 1999; Beck, McKeown, & Kucan, 2002). It leads to intrigue about what words

Words I love: grumpy, puke, slick, jelly, catamaran, teeth, pickle, elephant, jumble, oak

—Dylan

Words I love: laughter, disgusting, sunlight, horribly hot, glistening glitter, rocket ship, aliens, Neptune, orbit, temperature, shining light, starlight, Pluto, February, sweet, cheerful, creepy, mars, month/moon

—Kia

Words I love: destiny, mamamia, baboon, blunderbuss, pudgy, clergyman

—Morgan

**FIGURE 7-1**

*Best-loved words from students' notebooks*

can do. I encourage students to read the dictionary (yes, *read* it) and then notice and celebrate words they find when they show up in other books. I also encourage students to collect interesting words from their reading and jot them down in their writer's notebooks. (See Figure 7-1.) Writers must love words as much as painters love paint and musicians love notes.

If conversations around words happen continually in your classroom, you will surely come to love language. They will love words and combinations of words, and shades of meanings. They may also come to appreciate the richness of how words sound in other languages. Sometimes the essence of a thought can only be captured by a word in a student's native language, so we should allow a student to use it. However, I would encourage children to use those words sparingly and to italicize them so readers know they are borrowed from another language. Most of all, they will want to revise at the word level. So while you may have taught students to revise at the word level earlier in the year, don't stop. Extend and deepen the ways they can revise words. See Figure 7-2 for ideas.

## Revising at the Sentence Level

As much as writers love individual words, they also love the way words go together. When we teach students that words must go together to create graceful, fluid sentences, we move them forward in their writing. But we must teach them seriously. For example, we shouldn't simply tell students to vary sentence length and expect them to do it. We need to teach them that writers do this carefully and purposefully. They do not merely count words or alternate between one long and one short sentence. Students need demonstration and practice in composing sentences this way. (See Chapter 9.)

While words are the raw materials, sentences are the units of composition. The writer Cynthia Ozick (1990) claims she does not go on to write the next sentence until she is satisfied with first one. She understands the sentence captures a complete thought, and that writing is not just assembling random lovely words, but putting them together to convey meaning. It is said that a student once asked a well-known writer if he should be a writer. The writer replied, "Well, do you like sentences?" (Dillard, 1989).

# Ways to Deepen Revision at the Word Level

FIGURE 7-2

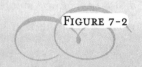

| SIMPLE REVISION STRATEGY | DEEPENING THE STRATEGY | EXAMPLES |
|---|---|---|
| Write in groups of three. | • Give each word a similar beginning sound.<br>• Give each word a similar, but more subtle sound.<br>• Give each word the same verb conjugation.<br>• Make each element the same grammatical structure, such as a prepositional phrase. | • Java is brown, brassy, and bold.<br>• He's ugly, cunning, and fun.<br>• Java is loping, jumping, panting.<br>• He jumped over the fence, into the pool, and under the float. |
| Use precise words. | • Use words from the list you've made in your notebook. Avoid the thesaurus.<br>• Use bland words when you don't want attention stolen from exciting words.<br>• Choose fewer words to describe something.<br>• Consider connotation as well as denotation. | • Java is wolfing with the neighbor's dog again.<br>• "Java, off to the pound with you," I said.<br>• "Get going!"<br>• He's slick and sly. |
| Repeat words and phrases thoughtfully. | Use repetition to create emphasis or cadence; repetition can be embedded over the length of a piece, as in a metaphor. | Java romps and rolls over the lawn toward a squirrel—romp and roll, romp and roll. |
| Elaborate on information. | Do not elaborate on every word or every sentence; use elaboration to capture the essence of something; include only details that will resonate with readers. | The man had hair poking out of his nose. (The reader doesn't need much more to get the picture.) |
| Consider the sounds of words. | Play with the words and the way they sound when read aloud; choose words in a row with the same numbers of syllables for certain effects, like moving fast in a story or bogging the reader down purposely. | I slid with the ice slicing my boot in two. |
| Use similes. | Use similes thoughtfully and sparingly; keep similes consistent in a piece; consider the sense of the mental picture you are drawing, e.g., don't make it humorous in a serious piece. | The dog was gentle as a stuffed bear. |
| Choose strong verbs and nouns. | Replace weak verbs and nouns with those that paint a picture. | Java sidled up to me, eyes begging for a cookie. "You sneak," I thought. |

The best way to teach students to write good sentences is to read aloud good examples so that students hear their music. I do not recommend teaching students about sentences the old-fashioned way, by dissecting them and labeling each part. It's too esoteric, at least for the students I've taught, not to mention boring. Students can get the "sense" of a sentence, of the concept of a complete thought, when we read it aloud and talk about what we notice.

I do not tell students to always write in complete sentences, because fragments can be used effectively, even by inexperienced writers. Plus, the books they read, presumably, contain many good, carefully placed fragments. We send a mixed message when we ask students to read good literature, but avoid trying the techniques of the authors of that literature. So let them write complete sentences and fragments in their notebooks for practice, find model sentences and fragments in mentor texts, and then talk about why writers might deliberately choose to write each one. There's one exception, though: state writing tests! For obvious reasons, it's wise to tell students that they should only write in complete sentences.

In Figure 7-3, I offer more ideas for helping students compose and combine sentences in effective ways. Another technique for teaching students to write more complicated sentences is to study a text one sentence at a time. See page 168 for a description of how one fourth-grade teacher did this.

## Revising at the "Chunk" Level

Teaching children to think about their fiction and nonfiction writing as chunks of information teaches them to categorize information as they plan their writing. It is also the best way to build paragraphing skills. It is almost impossible to go back to a solid mass of writing and break it into paragraphs if the information was not originally organized into discrete thoughts. Therefore, the most effective way to teach students to write in paragraphs is to teach them to chunk their information while planning. However, sometimes writers find they need to adjust the paragraphs once they've begun drafting, so they need to revise at the "chunk" level as well.

Teaching students to revise chunks prepares them to revise whole pieces. One way to help students revise individual chunks is to have them write the focus of their writing across the top of the page—for example, "what wolves eat"—and then compare each paragraph to the focus to make sure that they are including that information. This exercise also helps them to see if they are straying from

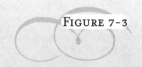

FIGURE 7-3

# Ways to Deepen Revision at the Sentence Level

| SIMPLE REVISION STRATEGY | DEEPENING THE STRATEGY | EXAMPLES |
|---|---|---|
| Write in sentences. | Use simple sentences only when you want to make something stand out, like the result of some action. Otherwise, use complex sentences. Use fragments sparingly for effect. | The brothers had both worked hard to bring that boat to shore, fighting the current and the storm. They were safe at last. Warm, dry, and safe. |
| Vary sentence length. | Vary length deliberately; read each sentence aloud for effect; vary the combinations of sentence structures. | Ellen clattered down the stairs, dropped her bags in the front hall, and bent to check if her CDs were packed. Where are they? she thought, where did I put them? I can't go without… "Let's go!" Dad was in a hurry. |
| Use a repeating sentence or rhythm to establish or maintain a mood or tone. | Use the repeating sentence as an organizer for sections of information. | • "I Have a Dream…"speech by Martin Luther King, Jr. • *Tough Boris* by Mem Fox: "He was scruffy. All pirates are scruffy." |
| Write believable dialogue. | Have characters speak in slang, with phrases they repeat, to communicate to others. | "No way!" Jimmy said. Mom frowned. "I am not kidding you. If you don't pass the test, you won't play basketball." "No way!" |
| Use punctuation to vary sentences. | Write a thought several times, varying punctuation; reread to test which comes closest to intended meaning. | I'm not interested in this! I'm not interested in…this. I'm—not interested in this. |
| Use some sentences to support others using topic statements and details. | Mark which sentences hold information that states a category and which hold details. | Wolves live in families similar to human families. They build homes to shelter their babies, they go out to get food for the young, and they even protect them from danger. |
| Write sentences in a logical order. | Be sure each sentence creates an expectation for the next one, so that the reader is pushed forward from one idea to the next. | Sometimes I like going to my grandmother's house. We play games together. She likes to play Scrabble and tic-tac-toe. But I like to play tag. That's when we don't agree and I want to go home. |

their topic or if they need more information to fill the chunk up. It is hard to revise for focus and organization if you cannot hold the logic of paragraphs in your mind, so this is one step on the way to wider revision. In Figure 7-4, I present more ideas for helping students revise chunks of text.

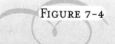

FIGURE 7-4

## Ways to Deepen Revision at the "Chunk" Level

| SIMPLE REVISION STRATEGY | DEEPENING THE STRATEGY | EXAMPLES |
|---|---|---|
| Find the greater meaning of your piece and write to it. | Use a controlling metaphor throughout the piece to illustrate your thinking. | In *Smoky Night* by Eve Bunting, two cats who usually fight become friends during a crisis. |
| Pan across the scene, then zoom in. | • Know the wider scene and the smaller details of it.<br>• Determine the main idea of each chunk and make sure that the details support it. | In *We Had a Picnic This Sunday Past* by Jacqueline Woodson, the family gathers for a reunion and anticipation builds for what one relative will do. |
| Decide on a logical order for your paragraphs. | • Imagine a different way to organize the chunks: Alternating points of view? Flashbacks? Withholding information to the end?<br>• Mix up the chunks, write each separately, then reassemble and look for surprise. | • In *White Socks Only* by Evelyn Coleman, the character tells the story through flashback.<br>• In *Home Place* by Crescent Dragonwagon, the character is imagining the entire story. |
| Find places where there is missing or extraneous information. | • "Tuck in" extra information (appositives) or build a new chunk around it.<br>• Write to include missing information, or rearrange what you have written to exclude it. | In *An Angel for Solomon Singer*, Cynthia Rylant uses commas and parentheses to tuck information into sentences. |

# PLANNING REVISION FOR THE REMAINDER OF THE YEAR

Once you have carried out a couple of units of study, and your students have a foothold on using revision strategies, keep the momentum going by incorporating more revision into subsequent units you plan. Revision strategies should be a part of every unit—and they should be cumulative as well. Be sure to encourage students not only to use strategies that you're currently teaching but also to continue to use strategies that you've taught them and those they've learned from mentor texts earlier in the year. That way, students are more likely to use the strategies automatically, confidently, and at the point of need.

Here's an example of what that might look like: Let's assume you have planned seven to ten units of study across the year, as well as several independent publications, in which students publish writing from their ongoing independent writing lives (Cruz, 2004). With all this writing, you provide many opportunities for students to practice revision. In addition, students use their writer's notebooks to practice revising regularly on short entries. Using the notebook as a place to try out strategies and play with writing is very effective.

Figure 7-5 shows a simple hypothetical yearlong plan for a writing curriculum that spells out a unit of study for each month and the accompanying revision strategies you might teach. (See Appendix F for one school's actual plan for the writing year.) Planning three or four strategy lessons in each unit, plus the revision work you do in small groups and individual conferences, provides your students with substantial direct instruction in revision. As they practice revising pieces on their own and with peers, applying what you've taught them, their skills will improve dramatically.

# A Yearlong Plan for a Writing Curriculum

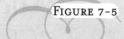 FIGURE 7-5

| TIME OF YEAR | UNIT OF STUDY | POSSIBLE BOTTOM-LINE REVISION STRATEGIES |
| --- | --- | --- |
| SEPTEMBER | Writerly life/Launching the writing workshop | • Keeping a writer's notebook<br>• Going through the writing process, including expectations for ongoing revision<br>• Establishing identity as a writer |
| OCTOBER | Personal narrative | • Determining significance<br>• Inserting purposeful dialogue<br>• Using images to create setting |
| NOVEMBER | Written conventions | • Using dashes to set off interrupted thoughts<br>• Using commas and a connecting word to put two sentences together<br>• Using quotation marks in dialogue and to insert an unusual word |
| DECEMBER | Personal essay | • Writing an ending that answers the beginning<br>• Including insights into situation<br>• Using selected details to support idea |
| JANUARY | Book review | • Including features of the genre: summary, commentary, connection to self<br>• Assuming detached voice of reviewer<br>• Embedding quotes |
| FEBRUARY | Report or feature article | • Ordering and grouping facts<br>• Deciding to get more information<br>• Using anecdote effectively |
| MARCH | Editorial | • Having a significant topic<br>• Using selected supporting facts<br>• Making opinion clear and precise |
| APRIL | Poetry | • Using some literary elements<br>• Choosing exact words<br>• Using poetic conventions (white space, line breaks) |
| MAY | Revision | Choose strategies based on assessment results. (See Chapter 10.) |
| JUNE | Writing projects or self-assigned writing based on interests | Revise your writing plan before you write (Murray's idea of "prewriting"). |

# Additional Deep Revision Strategies for Any Time of Year

Here are three revision strategies that are useful to students, regardless of the time of year or unit's topic: revising for genre, revising for voice, and revising for topic.

## Revising for Genre

Writers often try an idea in several different genres before they decide on the one that's right for the idea. Sometimes a story becomes a poem, for example, or a poem becomes an essay. They also combine genres—they write memoirs in a poetic form, for example, or embed personal narrative into editorials. So it makes sense to teach these strategies to students. Just be sure students can state clearly the genre or genres in which they are writing because they can use their knowledge of the features of that genre to help them write and revise.

Moving from one genre to another is a deep revision strategy that often involves rethinking the writing's basic idea and elements. For example, if I've written a story, I have characters, setting, and plot to help me get my idea across. Changing this story to a poem requires that I eliminate many words, concentrate more heavily on form, and possibly weave in literary devices such as metaphor. I'll have to suggest in a poem what I *stated explicitly* in a story. In order for students to do this, they need to study the genre to which they might switch, as well as find mentor authors. It's easier for young writers to move to a genre the class has already studied, but that may not always be possible. I would not discourage students from switching to an unfamiliar genre, but I would ask them to state their plans, as well as their ideas for finding mentor texts and learning about the new genre's features. If they seem to be on the right track, I would let them proceed.

## Revising for Voice

Donald Murray (1995) tells us that voice in writing is "what allows the reader's eyes to move over silent print and hear the writer speaking." It is the music of words and the personality of the writer coming through, and it makes the reader "trust you." Voice can be powerful, eccentric, academic, formal, ethnic, regional, individual, or businesslike. What it should not be is silent. Unfortunately, young writers sometimes struggle so hard with other facets of writing, such as finding a topic, adding details, and correcting spelling, that they have no energy for creating voice. However, revising gives them the perfect opportunity to let their voices be heard.

How can we do that? By looking to authors who do it well. Sharon Creech uses regional words and phrases, like *caboodle* and *gooseberry*, in *Walk Two Moons* to give it personality. Patricia Polacco uses a first-person narrative and a conversational tone. Gary Paulsen uses the short, clipped sentences we imagine that wilderness people might use. Cynthia Rylant uses unusual cadences (and punctuation to create them). Much writing for children contains a conversational, familiar tone that says to the reader, "Hey, pull up a chair. I've got something good to tell you."

THINGS I THINK ABOUT :

Can I change beginning or ending to be more purposeful ?
How would my favorite author do it → study his/her book
Do I have transition phrases ?
Is my purpose clear ?
What am I trying to say?

Revision Questions
1. Is the story interesting?
2. Does it make sense ?
3. Is it organized?
4. How can I expand?
5. Can I change any boring words to more description ones ?

Revising Questions for Conference

Who is my audience ?
Do I show the setting ok ?
Did I fold in information ?
Is the dialogue clear and real sounding ?

*Students grow as independent revisers by writing self-determined questions that drive their revision work.*

Yet often we discourage students from using their voices in writing. We teach them to avoid the "I" and instead embrace a feigned objective reserve. However, the best writing contains the writer's voice, even social studies reports and news articles. Students can look at writers they love and describe how those writers achieve voice in their writing. Even writing in an academic voice, such as in book reviews, involves using particular qualities to attain that distinct voice (Szczepanski, 2003). These include using appositives and writing long sentences, especially in book reviews.

Revising for voice involves reading texts aloud in many genres and thinking about how they sound. Students should listen for the *spoken quality* of the words. Better than the eye, the ear can pick up whether the writing sounds as if it were written by a human or a robot. From there, encourage students to apply what they hear to their own writing.

## Revising for Topic

Sometimes in the process of composing and rereading, a writer realizes that her topic has changed. It may have mysteriously strayed into a different topic, or the writer may have actually *discovered* a completely new topic. Sometimes the straying itself has some benefits because it requires the writer to make a choice whether to change her topic or stick with it. Usually the piece is muddy and unclear as it is and needs extensive work. For example, a child begins to write about her birthday party and, through writing her story, figures out that what she really wants to write about is how her brother always steals the show. Often a new insight like this one will make a student return to her notebook to work out the new topic.

## Maintaining Momentum

As students learn more about writing, their revisions will become more thoughtful and effective. We can help them gain independence by continuing the conversation about learning from mentor authors. But be aware that students may outgrow a mentor author. They may think they've learned all they can from Karen Hesse, and look around for another mentor author. At some point, they will probably return to Karen Hesse with wiser eyes, but it is good to find new authors to study—authors who will help students recognize and discover deep revisions on their own. Pushing oneself as a writer is a hard, but mature, thing to do.

It is just as important for us to continue to learn about writing and about revision. Often our biggest challenge is not the struggling student, because there is so much to teach her, but rather the student who writes so well *there seems to be nothing to teach him*. We might form study groups on this issue. We should also continue to find mentor authors. Or we can read books about writing and revision, because they are filled with wonderful ideas for professional writers. Using these ideas with the whole class, in small groups, or in individual conferences shows all students ways to revise deeply and pushes those who are ready for a challenge.

# SUMMARY

Planning for revision in every unit of study sends a message that revision is important all year and in every genre. In addition, pushing students toward making deeper and more extensive revisions broadens their knowledge base and gives them a bigger menu of options for improving their work. We want students to revise automatically and to think about revision while composing, as well as when they're finished composing. Rereading their drafts with a revision focus is a powerful way to guide students toward better writing.

## Some Points to Remember

- Once students feel comfortable with a number of simple revision strategies, you can push them further by extending and refining each one.

- Deep revision can happen at the word level across an entire piece.

- The degree of the reviser's sophistication determines whether he is ready for deep revision.

- Some deep revision should be required at some point from every student.

- Students should read mentor authors to find ideas for deep revision.

- Deep revision may take days, and in that time the writer's genre and/or topic could change.

- Show students that making wise decisions on deep revisions may require multiple rereadings, each with a specific type of deep revision in mind.

# CHAPTER EIGHT

# REVISITING PUBLISHED PIECES IN A REVISION UNIT OF STUDY

Not long ago, I wrote a short memoir as I worked with some students in Canada. At the time, I liked the memoir very much; in fact, I was quite pleased with myself as a writer. When I picked it up again three months later, I was horrified. It was trite, predictable, and melodramatic. Frankly, it was awful. But the distance of time made the realization less painful because I was no longer in love with my piece, as if it were a child I had birthed. Time had given me the objectivity I needed to revise ruthlessly and effectively.

Many writers advise us to take time off from a piece of writing. For example, Toni Morrison (1998) says, "You have to learn how to read your work; I don't mean enjoy it because you wrote it. I mean, go away from it, and read it as though it is the first time you've ever seen it. Critique it that way. Don't get all involved in your thrilling sentences." When writing has just flowed from our brains and hearts, we often can't see its flaws: places where the words sound awkward, the organization doesn't work, the focus is unclear, and so on. It's as if love for our sentences—fancy words, a turn of phrase—clouds our judgment. We can't see where the writing falls short of its original purpose, where it's unclear or predictable, or whether it works at all. That's why Stephen Koch (2003) recommends a "decent cooling period," after which you should "read with the detachment of a doctor reading X-rays... You'll come across lots of things that will make you want to scream. Sloppiness. Stupid blunders. Incomprehensible passages. Boring passages. Embarrassments."

Writers can do a lot to save a piece by giving the writing a rest and then going back to it to revise. Therefore, I like to plan a unit of study in revision— a unit where the only thing students do is revise. No writing new pieces. No impressing us with finished or newly composed stories. Just revision. For this unit, students revise a piece they've published to feel what it's like to revisit writing after time has passed. It makes sense to schedule this unit late in the school year, so students have many writing pieces from which to choose. Often students want to revise a piece they wrote back in October or November. Because so much time has passed, they can see many ways to revise it. They see how much they've learned as writers and how they can use their writing and revising skills to make their writing better.

In this chapter I examine a unit of study on revision. In some ways, this unit is advanced work. However, if we've been continually teaching revision all year, students will be ready for more sophisticated techniques. I look at

- building and maintaining strength in revision

- planning a unit of study

- carrying out the unit, day by day

- encouraging independent inquiry into revision

# Building and Maintaining Strength in Revision

Several years ago, Philip Levine, a fifth-grade teacher at Main Street School in Irvington, New York, wrote a short memoir while he was part of a teachers' after-school writing group. He used that memoir in class to demonstrate the steps of his writing process, from entries in his notebook to his first draft and subsequent revisions. He referred to the piece all year long and used his work as a teaching tool when it made sense to do so.

However, that came to an end when he and I met with other teachers last spring to discuss using mentor texts in a revision unit of study. (See Figure 8-1 for how the Main Street teachers fit this unit into their end-of-the-year plan.) Phil talked about his favorite mentor text, *Grandpa's Face*, by Eloise Greenfield. As we talked, a thoughtful look came over Phil's face. "You know," he said, "I wrote my memoir almost ten years ago, and I think it's pretty good. But now, as I look at Greenfield's work, I see a few things I would want to change in it, a couple of things I could make better... even though I think it's fine now!"

We all laughed. Certainly Phil's writing is fine, but with the distance of time and the knowledge of a mentor author, he saw that there were things he could've revised. So Phil went through Greenfield's text and highlighted craft decisions she made, then he went through his own writing to make corresponding changes.

|  |  | | | | | | | | | | |
|---|---|---|---|---|---|---|---|---|---|---|---|
| *Curriculum Plan for Main Street School* **Writing** | | | | | | | | | | | |
|  | **Unit 1** | **Unit 2** | **Unit 3** | **Unit 4** | **Unit 5** | **Unit 6** | **Unit 7** | **Unit 8** | **Unit 9** | **Unit 10** |
| **Grade 4** | Assessment, Launch the writing workshop | Personal narrative | Improving the Quality of Student Writing: Conventions | Responding to Literature | Writing for the ELA | Poetry | Nonfiction Writing: Feature Article | Realistic Fiction using Mentor Authors | Assessment/ Revision and reflection | Writing Projects |
| **Dates** | Sept. | Oct. | Nov. | Dec. | Jan. | Feb. | March – mid-April | End of April – May | June | June |
| **Grade 5** | Assessment, Launch the writing workshop | Conventions | Essay on content area material | Realistic Fiction | Book Review | Poetry | Digging Deeper: notebooks and revision OR writing about reading | Persuasive Or Literary Essay (based on social issue book clubs) | Historical Fiction *or* Personal Narrative | Revision Reflection and/or Writing Projects |
| **Dates** | Sept. | Oct. – 2 weeks | Mid-Oct. thru Nov | Dec. | Jan. 3 weeks | Jan. 1 wk Feb. 2-3 weeks | March | April | May | June |

**Figure 8–1**

*One school's at-a-glance year-long plan for writing*

Phil planned to use these changes as the basis for modeling how writers see new things to revise when returning to a piece after time. (See Figure 8-2.)

A unit of study on revision is a good unit to teach in late spring, when students' folders are bulging with writing to revise. The purpose is to teach students to reread their writing with critical eyes and revise accordingly. Returning to a

**Philip Levine: Revisions I decided to make in my memoir after studying Grandpa's Face by Eloise Greenfield**

- Work on dialogue that shows the character's emotions
- Stay deep in the moment of the story
- Use physical behavior to show the character's feelings
- Shop around for better words
- Make each character seem different and more real – write fewer characters and make them individual thro
- Figure out something original to say
- Invent the truth (learned from William Z everything that really happened, but twe

FIGURE 8-2

*One teacher's revision of his writing after studying* Grandpa's Face *by Eloise Greenfield.*

The Saddest Night of My Life

by Mr. Philip Levine

On a Thursday night in the summer of '86, I said good-bye to a friend. I will never forget that night. Gibby, a husky jet black Labrador retriever, and I grew up together.

She acquired her nickname, Gibby, the day we got her. I was twelve. My sister Randi only nine. We refused to acknowledge that our dog would grow up being called Gibora; the name chosen by Mom. Gibora is the literal English translation of the Hebrew word heroine. How appropriate! For fifteen years, Gibby was my solid companion. Her physical abilities, good nature and determination were of heroic proportions.

Growing up, I clearly recall Gibby tearing down the hallway. Sliding on wooden floors like a hockey puck on ice, but always remaining steady on her feet. Numerous times in the beautiful forests of Harriman State Park, I tried to outrun and hide from her yet always failed. Gibby snatched tossed balls with the ease of a superior athlete leaping to grasp a long fly baseball.

Throughout high school and college vacations, she patiently waited through countless card games. Our "security guard" accepted laughter and bad jokes like a true champ. She never complained. Smiles with a wet tongue always greeted me upon tiptoeing upstairs in the early morning hours.

Gibby always made me smile. After hearing the word "kennel", her ears shot up like a miniature jack-in-the-box and her tail mimicked a canoe being tossed about in a water rapid. This was her response to an upcoming ride in the car. The day she hurled herself into Cousin Elenor's pool I loved her even more. She maneuvered around the pool like a seal in the rocky waters of Monterey. Gibby was beautiful slopping up water from her gray mixing bowl and stealing slices of steak from Dad's plate. Her appetite and persistence were endless.

I can recall the Thursday night I arrived at 5 Wood Lane like last night. On Saturday, a veterinarian was going to put Gibby to sleep. Mom and Dad would be with her but I would not. Thursday night would be the last time I could grab hold of her muscular neck and front legs, wrestle her to the ground and rest my head against her stomach like one does with a broken in pillow.

As I walked into the kitchen area, I eyed Gibby next to the rectangular glass table. Somehow she was always capable of plopping herself down within the table's brass frame. She looked so peaceful, so content. Instinctively I yelled, "Gibby, what's up?" No response. Her hearing was nil. If Gibby wasn't awake she was oblivious to the world around.

## Teaching Students to Watch Themselves as Thinkers and Revisers

It's important for students to understand how they write and how they revise—in other words, to watch themselves as thinkers and revisers (Horning, 2004). So you might want to begin this unit by asking them, "What do you do when you revise?" Many students will tell you that they don't know what they do; they've never stepped back to watch themselves. This happens with students who have very little knowledge of revision as well as with students who have a lot. But once you teach them to watch themselves as thinkers and revisers, they realize that they have certain habits as they revise—they may read their writing through with no intention or questions in mind, or they skim, or they try to get it right the first time, or they have no energy for revising, and so on. Their answers will give you lots of information from which to teach. Once you know what they do, you can teach them to maintain or alter their behaviors.

past piece can teach students some powerful truths about writing:

- We are never really "done" with writing.

- We change as writers as we read books and study writing.

- The more we write, the more we learn about writing.

- We can use revision strategies we already know to revise ruthlessly because we're no longer emotionally attached to this writing.

- We can keep mining texts by mentor authors to learn more about writing and revising.

Students develop sophistication about revision; in a unit dedicated to revision they get to step back and choose from the entire menu of strategies they know in order to find the ones that work best in a particular piece of writing. Our job is to guide them to make the best decisions. Often young writers think they have to apply all revision strategies in every piece of writing they produce. When we layer on strategy after strategy all year long, we run the risk of making students loathe writing and revision. But knowing how to choose the right strategies to move a piece closer to the writer's vision can prevent that. It is a sophisticated and important skill. Later in the chapter, I show you how to build it.

During a unit of study in revision, you can begin your final assessment about what students have learned by observing them, conferring with them, and examining their writing. Assessment of student work can also cast light on our teaching. If students are unable or unwilling to revise after nearly an entire year of instruction, we need to reassess *how we are teaching them* to do it.

Elise

I am learning to play the guitar.
My teacher is nice and plays rea...
to play rock and roll music and b...
best friend Shelley and I want...
Guitar is hard but I like it.

Tell a story → practicing since I got a guita...

REVISIONS

- Transition words
- Precise words
- Elaboration

A student makes revision plans independently.

Elise

Ever since I saw MTV I wanted to be a famous rock star. ⓣ Last Christmas, the biggest present of all under the tree was mine. It was a shiny new guitar. ⓣ Since then, I have tried to practice every day but it was hard to learn to play because I didn't have anyone to teach me. Two weeks ago, I started lessons with a really ⓟ patient, kind teacher. Sometimes he ⓔ plays the music to show me how it should sound and he's really ⓟ amazing. I think he should be famous.

My best friend Shelley is learning to play the drums and we want to start a band. ⓔ We have sleepovers and talk all night about what songs we can play in our band. Learning guitar is harder than I thought it would be but my teacher says if I keep ⓔ practicing I'll get much better quickly. I can't wait to get as good as he is so I can be famous. I just wish my fingers didn't hurt so much!

ⓣ = I used transition words.
ⓟ = I used precise words.
ⓔ = I elaborated.

During the unit, students can also reflect on how they've grown as writers and make plans for future work. They can use revision ideas they've gotten from mentor authors all year long. They can focus on revision without going through the entire writing process and writing a new draft.

# PLANNING A UNIT OF STUDY

Here is the overall structure for unit of study on revision, designed to take place over three weeks. The revision work that students do will come from what you choose to teach, based on what you feel your students need, and from their independent study of mentor authors.

# Week 1

To begin the unit, tell students:

- Reread all published pieces in their entirety without judgment or criticism. Although it may be tempting to marvel at some pieces and scoff at others, refrain from making snap judgments. You need to remain objective to identify good writing and bad writing.

- Make margin notes where the writing might be improved. (See Figure 8-3.) Do not revise at this point, though.

- Decide on one long piece or two short pieces that have potential for some new, interesting, and possibly major revision. Challenge yourself to grow, rather than choosing an easy piece to revise.

- Make a list of revision strategies you already know that could work with the piece.

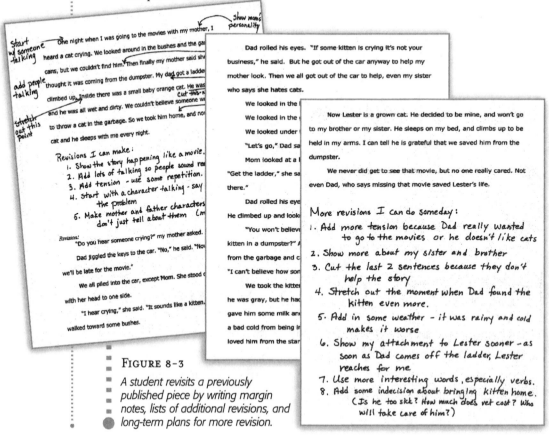

FIGURE 8-3

*A student revisits a previously published piece by writing margin notes, lists of additional revisions, and long-term plans for more revision.*

## Week 2

Begin targeted instruction on new revision strategies. (See mini-studies later in this chapter.) Then tell students:

- Meet with writing partners to discuss the revisions you are contemplating and to get other ideas for revising this piece.

- Write a short paragraph about what already works in the writing and why you think certain parts need revision.

- Meet in small writing groups to imagine ways to revise other pieces, making photocopies for all group members, if possible.

- Use the teacher's revision lessons to find new ways to revise the piece.

- Keep double-sided entries in your notebook, recording the types of revisions you have made on one side of the page and reflections on how effective or successful they were on the other.

## Week 3

Tell students:

- Practice thinking like a reviser by planning deep revisions; then do some of those revisions on the piece you chose.

- Look at your mentor author to get ideas for ways to revise; this will build independence in finding ways to revise writing.

- Mark your revisions on your draft by underlining or highlighting them. Then record your thinking and decision-making in the margin, so you know why you revised as well as what the revision was. Refer to mentor authors if appropriate.

- Reflect on what you've learned about yourself as a reviser and how you can push yourself to grow more.

- Celebrate by sharing several of your best revision decisions with classmates.

---

### Seemingly Small, But Powerful, Revision Strategies

**Delete words and phrases that have little meaning** (for example: *at this point in time, kind of, particular, basically, various, the story I'm going to tell you is,* and *now you know why*)

**Delete phrases that can be inferred** (for example: *anticipate in advance*) **or seem redundant** (for example: *the big mansion, the ugly monster*)

**Reduce phrases to words** (for example: *at this point in time* to *now*)

**Change negatives to positives** (for example: *I don't remember* to *I forget*)

Some students will not understand your purpose for this unit. "More revisions? We already revised these pieces!" In conferences or small groups, you can help them see additional work they can do on one or two pieces and the benefit of using their notebooks to reflect on their work. At the end of the unit, students publish their newly revised pieces.

Depending on the extent of work each piece needed at the start, the amount of revision will vary. Some pieces will remain the same in terms of topic, genre, and qualities of writing but read much better. Others may seem like completely new pieces because of the revision discoveries students made in the unit. What's important is not *how much* students revised, but *how* and *why* they revised. Encourage them to read their "before" and "after" pieces and share their decisions with the class.

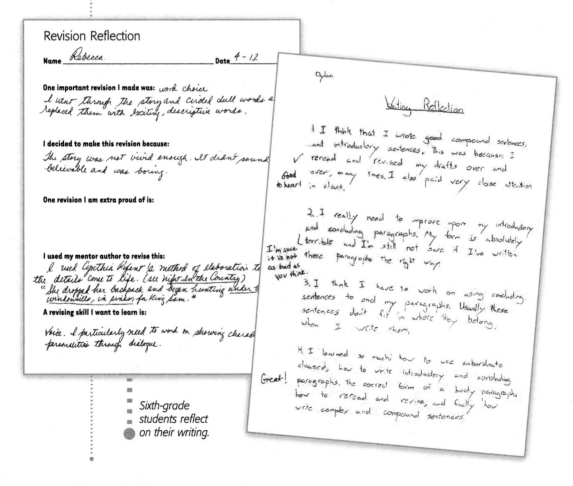

Sixth-grade students reflect on their writing.

The effective reviser learns to look outside himself to consider his readers. He understands that he is writing for others, as well as himself, and that in order to reach his readers, he must be sensitive to their needs. The object of revision becomes the reader, not the writer. "Will my reader get this?" should pervade the writer's mind while revising, not "If my reader doesn't get this, it's just too bad." Understanding the reader drives the reviser to go on, which is why this unit works best in late spring. At that point, presumably, students have grasped the importance of audience.

# CARRYING OUT THE UNIT, DAY BY DAY

The following three mini-studies represent what you might teach in the second week of the sample unit just described. Although I'm suggesting one mini-study per week, you might choose to do two over three weeks if one per week is too much for your students. Alternately, you may do only one mini-study for the entire unit and devote more time to helping students find new mentor authors for revision.

Each mini-study focuses on an important aspect of writing—organization, genre, and point of view, and therefore students get targeted teaching. However, you might find that your students need something quite different. If so, use these mini-studies as inspiration to aspects of writing where your students need work. Remember, these are only suggestions for mini-studies within the unit on revision.

## Writing Groups in the Classroom

Adult writers often meet regularly with other writers in small groups, with members committed to each helping one another improve their writing. Groups usually convene every week or twice a month, and work best when all members feel comfortable and when there is a sense of trust.

Classroom writing groups can work the same way. Have interested students meet in groups of no more than four on a regular basis to give and receive feedback on writing. Students should go to the group with a piece of writing, questions about their writing, and a photocopy of the piece for each member. Before they meet, teach students positive ways to respond to each other, specifically how to criticize without being hurtful and to think of constructive ideas for revision. Also, allow students to practice *taking* criticism graciously and disagreeing politely. Finally, assess each group's work and effectiveness by observing group meetings, conferring with the group, and requiring students to fill out a short form that details their work at the end of each meeting.

# Mini-Study on Revising for Organization

## DAY 1

**TEACHING POINT:** Sometimes writers investigate deeply a single option for organizing writing.

**WHOLE-CLASS WORK:** Look at a class mentor text together to figure out the author's rationale for organization. Draw boxes around major parts, summarize them, and determine how they're organized—chronologically? in order of importance? in flashback or flash-forward?

**STUDENT WORK:** Do the same thing with one of your drafts. If you can't determine how the piece is organized, study it further to figure why the organization isn't working. Make plans to change it.

## DAY 2

**TEACHING POINT:** Sometimes writers investigate many options for organizing writing.

**WHOLE-CLASS WORK:** Talk to students about all the options writers have for organizing writing. They may state something, give examples, and then come back to reexamine the original statement, as in *Wolves* by Seymour Simon. Another option is to take the reader on a journey that is framed by the movement of time, as in *Night in the Country*, by Cynthia Rylant. I organized my memoir on finding my cat in a Dumpster by framing it according to my changing emotions. When I look at one of my mentor authors, Karen Hesse, I notice that many of her stories are framed by a central event that propels the action forward, such as in *Come On, Rain!*, where the characters wait for the rain and enjoy it when it comes.

**STUDENT WORK:** Try playing with the organization of your piece by using an idea from your mentor author. Be able to say what the organizing option is.

## DAY 3

**TEACHING POINT:** Sometimes writers find a way to organize their writing that they really like. It is comfortable to them, so they use it again and again. This is usually effective, but sometimes it can be confining and make the writing predictable.

So it's not always a good idea. It's important to examine whether we are using a structure out of habit or because it really works.

**WHOLE-CLASS WORK:** Study a few mentor texts by one author to determine the kind of organizer he or she is. Does he or she tend to use the same structure or does he or she choose structures specifically to fit each piece?

**STUDENT WORK:** Look at all your drafts to analyze the organizational structures you tend to use. Write each structure on a sticky note and put it on each draft. Then consider whether you used the best structure for each draft or whether you used it because it is comfortable, and how some of the drafts might work better if organized differently.

# Mini-Study on Revising for Genre

### DAY 1

**TEACHING POINT:** Sometimes writers revise to make the writing fit their chosen genre better.

**WHOLE-CLASS WORK:** Show students a piece of writing in need of genre revision and think aloud this way: At this point in the year, we've learned about several genres of writing, including poetry, feature articles, and book reviews. (See Figure 7-5 for a sample curriculum calendar.) Now that we know so much about genres, we can look back at our drafts and find places where our writing did not quite fulfill the promise of the genre. For example, I wrote a realistic fiction story. When I look at the chart we made when we studied realistic fiction, I see that one important characteristic of that genre is that some kind of change takes place in the story, whether it is a change in the main character or a solution to the conflict in the story. As I look back at the story I wrote, I see that the change was minor and had no significance at all. (See Figure 8-4.) So I will go back and rethink my entire story to see how I could make the change in the main character more significant. This may mean I have to rework a large part of my story, but that's okay. I am revising to make my story closer to the characteristics of the genre in which I wrote.

**STUDENT WORK:** Choose one piece you wrote this year and compare it to the class chart of the characteristics of that genre. If your writing doesn't contain those characteristics, revise it.

# Revising Stories to Amplify Change

FIGURE 8-4

## FIRST DRAFT #1

When I went to the pet store, I saw three puppies I liked. There was a gray one, and two poodles. I held all three of them and I couldn't decide which one I wanted. Then I asked my mother which one I could have, and she said I couldn't have any of them. We were just looking. I started to cry. Then we left the store.

In this version, the character didn't change at all. He just registered disappointment. This is a fine notebook entry, but not good as a story, because the character should change in a story.

### Revision

When I went to the pet store, I saw three puppies I liked. I knew we were just there to buy fish food. My mother said to leave the puppies alone, but I played with them anyway. There was a gray one and two poodles. I held all of them, and I imagined that I could have all three. I pretended I could walk them and feed them and they could sleep in my bed.

Then I asked my mother if I could have one, and she shook her head. I knew the answer already. "The landlord doesn't allow pets." I started to cry even though I knew it wasn't anyone's fault I couldn't have them.

I kissed each one of them and put them back in the cages. Someday I will find a way to have a dog, I thought.

In this version, the character comes to realize that he can't have what he wants, but he can make plans for the future. This character has changed by coming to understand a situation that looks hopeless to him.

## FIRST DRAFT #2

Every Friday in school we have ice cream at lunch. I like ice cream. I like vanilla and chocolate. Sometimes I eat vanilla. Sometimes I eat chocolate. I never say no, and I always eat the ice cream.

In this version, the choice the character must make is not critical to the story. It makes no difference which one he chooses, so there is no tension in the story.

### Revision

Every Friday in school we have ice cream at lunch. I really love ice cream, but I am lactose intolerant. If I eat it, I get really sick. So when the lunch lady asks me if I want vanilla or chocolate, I have to say no. Sometimes I feel the word "Chocolate" pop out of my mouth. Then I take the ice cream to my seat and watch it melt in the dish. I want to eat it so bad, but I know I can't.

One day my friend Annamarie made fun of me for not eating it. She said it was stupid not to eat ice cream and there was no such thing as being allergic to it. I felt really bad. I just decided I didn't care if I got sick, so I ate it.

That afternoon I got really sick. The teacher had to call my mother to take me home. I won't listen to Annamarie ever again.

The character's choice presents some consequences for her. The character is changed by making the wrong choice and learns something from her mistake.

## DAY 2

**TEACHING POINT:** Often one revision leads to others.

**WHOLE-CLASS WORK:** Show students a revised piece of writing in need of further revision and think aloud this way: I am thinking about that story I mentioned earlier, where the main character's change was not significant. I'm revising to fix that, but now I've noticed another problem: the story doesn't fulfill the promise of its genre. My character has a pretty big problem now—he's baby-sitting for his little sister and an intruder is trying to break in—but he is not the one who solves the problem. In the end, his parents come home, and so they solve the problem for him. My story would be so much stronger if I could figure out a way for my main character to solve the problem. So I'm going to do another major revision.

**STUDENT WORK:** Study your own draft to see if one revision has made it necessary for you to change something else, and if there are more characteristics of the genre that you can incorporate.

## DAY 3

**TEACHING POINT:** Writers try a solution to the conflict in a story many different ways until they find one that works.

**WHOLE-CLASS WORK:** Show students a piece of writing in need of revision and think aloud this way: I've been trying to work out how to help my main character solve his problem, but it's just not working out. I went back to my mentor text, *The Whipping Boy*, and I've thought a lot about it. I wonder if Sid Fleischman had trouble finding a way for Jemmie to solve his problem. It seems he gave Jemmie such a big problem that it would be hard for him to solve it. So I imagine that maybe Sid made a list of all the ways that Jemmie might solve the problem, and then he tried writing each one until he found one that works. That's how I'm going to find a way for my character to solve his problem.

**STUDENT WORK:** Make a list of several ways to solve the main character's problem in your story, or imagine how your mentor author would have solved it. Then try out some of those possibilities in your notebook until you find one that works.

# Mini-Study on Revising for Point of View

### DAY 1

**TEACHING POINT:** Writers choose carefully which character will tell their story.

**WHOLE-CLASS WORK:** Show students a piece of first-person writing in need of revision and think aloud this way: When I study mentor authors, I see that there are many options for who will narrate the story. Sometimes the story is being told by the main character in his or her voice, as in *Come On, Rain!* by Karen Hesse. If I write using the "I" voice, I can really let my personality show; but I cannot know what is happening in anyone's mind except my own. I noticed that when I wrote my memoir, I kept telling what my daughter was thinking during the story. Well, that's silly, because I am not inside her head, so I cannot know exactly what she is thinking. I can only see what she's doing and how her face, body, and talking reveal what she's thinking. So now I'm going to go back and revise my memoir so that I'm only telling what I am thinking. I will use Cheryl's actions to tell what may be going on inside her head.

**STUDENT WORK:** If you have written in the first person, be sure that you describe only your own emotions and what is going on inside your head. If you have not written any pieces in the first person this year, revise a piece to tell the story in the "I" voice.

### DAY 2

**TEACHING POINT:** Writers maintain a consistent point of view. Even when they're not writing in the first person, writers are careful to avoid writing from inside more than one character's head because it confuses the reader.

**WHOLE-CLASS WORK:** Show students a piece of writing in need of revision because it contains multiple perspectives, and think aloud this way: When I was looking at one of my mentor texts for the story, *The Whipping Boy*, I noticed that the "person" telling the story is not a character in the story at all. He's someone else, called a narrator, who is watching it all happen and reporting it to us. Nevertheless, he seems to know what's going on in the main character's head; for the rest of the characters, he reports only their actions.

When I wrote my story, I told what each of the characters was thinking, and now I realize that this is confusing to the reader. It's as if I was inside everyone's head, which is ridiculous. So now I'm going to revise my story to make sure that I am telling it from one point of view.

**STUDENT WORK:** If you try to tell what's happening in every character's mind, you will lose control of your story and your focus. Revise some writing today to be sure you have a clear sense of what the character telling the story can and can't tell. Be sure you choose a point of view and you stay with it.

## DAY 3

**TEACHING POINT:** Writers have ways to give readers information about secondary characters without jumping into their heads to tell us what they are thinking.

**WHOLE-CLASS WORK:** Show students a piece of writing in need of revision because its supporting characters are not described well, and think aloud this way: I've been reading very carefully to see how writers tell us about the supporting characters in books, and I've noticed that they do a couple of things. One is that they allow the main character to describe the supporting characters. In other places, the writer tells us what the secondary characters are doing, or saying, or how emotions show on their faces or their bodies. Let's look at how Sid Fleischman does this. He has Jemmie tell us about the other characters. Today I'm going to revise my story to give my readers information about my supporting characters by using one of the other ways that writers do it.

**STUDENT WORK:** Choose one of the ways writers tell us about their supporting characters, and revise some writing using it.

# Other Possible Mini-Studies for a Revision Unit of Study

Using the qualities of good writing as a framework, you can design other mini-studies to teach within your revision unit of study. Knowing what your students need helps you make wise decisions. Here are some ideas:

- Rewrite the same piece for several different audiences (my article about wolves for readers of *Ranger Rick*, the National Rifle Association, and *The New Yorker*)

- Cut or trim unnecessary passages, sentences, phrases, words

# Possible Mini-Lessons for a Revision Unit of Study

| WHAT TO TEACH | HOW TO TEACH IT |
|---|---|
| Find something new to learn from your mentor author and write out what it is in the margins of your writing. | Demonstrate seeing something "new" in a text you have been using all year. Rereading a well-known text slowly can reveal new things. |
| Ask another writer in the class to recommend a new mentor author in order to search for new things to do. | Demonstrate needing or wanting to do something very different in your writing or being unable to find an answer in your mentor author. |
| Read your writing aloud (in a murmur). Use your ear from our read-alouds to listen to the music of your sentences: rhythm, cadence, and transitions. | Read your own writing aloud while showing it on a transparency. Model hearing where it sounds awkward, harsh, or rough, and where the reader is confused because transitions are unclear. |
| Reread your writing to decide if it really fits in the genre you wrote it in. | Model rereading your piece, e.g., a memoir, and thinking how it might work as a poem or essay; then try out some phrases and plan to start drafting in that direction. |
| Reread for authenticity. | Is the information in the piece true? Does the dialogue sound like real people talking? Are the characters doing things that real people would do? Demonstrate finding places in your writing where the information doesn't ring true. |
| Reread for clarity. | Have I used too many words to say something? Have I said too much? Do my sentences go in circles? Have I used specific words? Can I see the story in my mind as it is happening? Do I leave too much work to my reader? Show places where one or more of these things have happened in your writing. |
| Reread to see if the writing is interesting. | Is my story compelling? Why would my reader care? How can I make him care? Do I have to elaborate or cut in order to interest my reader? |
| Reread for point of view. | Model in your own writing: Have I switched the person who is telling the story? Did I pop inside too many characters' heads? Who is the one person telling this story and have I kept it that way? |

- Redefine the purpose of my writing; make sure I fulfill my promise to readers

- Clarify voice, perhaps by making it stronger or changing it from detached to "in your face" strong personality writing

- Maintain focus and balance in writing

- Use details sparingly and appropriately; use details to reveal character

- Develop your own style

- Study beginnings that start in the middle of the action; write endings that satisfy the reader

- Prepare a manuscript for submission to real-world markets

# ENCOURAGING INDEPENDENT INQUIRY INTO REVISION

The key to teaching students to be independent is to teach them to read deeply (Cruz, 2004; Nia, in press). Most readers do not know how to step back from a text to see exactly what the writer has done. But when we teach students to do that, we give them the keys to independence. They need never again be confused because now they know *how* to look in texts to find answers to questions about writing. Showing students how to read texts for answers is like showing a beginning baseball player how to study Derek Jeter's moves; that young player can figure out answers to baseball questions, even if there is no one to ask.

Therefore, during a revision unit, we should ask students to find a text they have not studied before and to mine it for new ideas. You might ask students to tell you three to five new revision strategies they discover and to indicate where they tried some of them.

## Keys to Helping Students Become Independent Revisers

Here are three things students need to move toward revision independence.

**TRUSTED PARTNERS:** having the frequent opportunity to bounce ideas off peers and receive feedback

**A BANK OF STRATEGIES:** seeing revisions that work in writing and developing a bank of strategies to rely on.

**MENTOR AUTHORS:** knowing how to read texts, looking for writing answers, and having a knowledge of some worthwhile texts to study

As part of the revision unit, you may also want to teach students to reflect on their work as writers and revisers. Metacognition—knowing who we are and how we think—is a powerful tool for pushing our learning forward. Just as I know myself as a person who consumes way too much chocolate, I know myself as a writer who writes too many extra words and needs to go back and revise them.

Talking with partners and comparing writing to mentor texts can open a window into types of unproductive revision trends each writer encounters. Students discover these trends through long-term revision. You can provide tools to help them identify what to work on quickly, such as the chart in Figure 8-5. (See Appendix D for a reproducible version of this chart.)

| Revision Trend | Example from My Writing | My Revised Writing | Plan for My Future Writing |
|---|---|---|---|
| I start too slow. | I got up and got dressed. Then I combed my hair and brushed my teeth. Then I went to breakfast and my father said let's go to the beach. | One morning during breakfast, my dad said, "Let's go to the beach." | Keep my reader's interest by getting into my story faster. |
| I use ordinary words. | I like my brother. He is a good brother and he is fun. | I am stuck to my brother like glue. When I'm with him, we laugh and play tricks all day. | Write with details because that will make me write more interesting words. |

FIGURE 8-5

*A student uncovers recurring revision trends in his writing and makes plans to avoid them.*

Students begin to see trends in their writing, both good and bad, if you give them the opportunity to study their writing (Shaughnessy, 1977). Ask them to choose several pieces from their folders and notebook entries, and then lay them out on the table. If your students are sophisticated revisers, they will be able to look at these pieces and notice two things: things they do over and over and types of revisions they have to make consistently. For younger or less sophisticated students, you may have to do this work for them. For example, Freddy's teacher, Mary Jane O'Brien, asks her fourth-grade students to look in their writing for five things:

1. Types of words they use

2. Ways they begin their writing

3. Endings that truly complete the story

4. Complete sentences

5. Varied sentence lengths

Freddy identifies two revision trends in his writing (i.e., things he will look for every time he revises). As the week continues, the students identify one trend in their writing that they've discovered on their own. (See Figure 8-6.)

I never put in what I'm thinking and I should do that.

I jumble all my facts together. I should think about
how they go together in groups.

I repeat the same things using different words to try to make my
writing longer. I have to plan my writing better so I have more to say.

My sentences all sound the same. I should write in my notebook to
practice writing sentences in long and short ways.

I use the same words over and over. I should find some new words
to use by looking in the books I like to read.

FIGURE 8-6

*What fourth graders say about
their revision needs*

This kind of self-awareness, or "meta-rhetorical awareness," supports students' independence in writing long after they are finished with their assignments. It also supports their learning capacity because knowing what they need to work on and having a plan for doing it is liberating and powerful.

# SUMMARY

Students need to know how to revise quickly. After all, there are times when they'll need to think and work on their toes (when they take the SATs, for example). But they also deserve to learn long-term revision. Giving them the opportunity to work deeply on revision will help them become better writers. They will develop the ability to recognize the types of revision they need to do through practicing many revision strategies. A revision unit of study teaches students the power of letting a piece of writing rest for awhile and then going back to it to apply everything they've learned since they put it down.

## Some Points to Remember

- Students need time to plan revisions and reflect on past writing during a revision unit of study.

- The purpose of the unit is not to produce a new piece of writing; however, students may revise an old piece to a point where it seems new.

- Students need to become independent and have intentions as they revise.

- Students should be encouraged to create a bank of revision strategies to draw upon, and be given opportunities to practice strategies until they can apply them automatically.

- Students must always push themselves to figure out new ways to revise.

# CHAPTER NINE

# Using Punctuation and Grammar as Revision Tools

Liz was the best writer in my eighth-grade class. Whether she was tackling a story, an essay, or a play, her writing was always compelling. One afternoon, she asked me to comment on an eight-page story she had written. I was delighted to, until I sat down to read it that evening and was shocked to discover that Liz had not used any punctuation! When I asked her about it the next day, she said with a giggle, "Oh, Ms. A., you're so good at it that I figured you could just put it in wherever you wanted it!"

Clearly my teaching had failed her. Liz was a fine writer who had not yet learned—despite all the worksheets and drill I provided—that writers use punctuation to compose with meaning. She assumed that punctuation was something that only the teacher valued, so the teacher might as well plug it in wherever she felt it needed to go. Punctuation was just a bunch of rules to Liz.

In my three years as her English teacher (sixth through eighth grade), I had not taught Liz or any of my students the beauty of a well-placed comma or a thoughtfully used dash. Pico Iyer (1996) says in his lovely essay "In Praise of the Humble Comma": "Punctuation is a matter of care... care for words, yes, but also, and more important, for what the words imply... No iron can pierce the heart with such force as a period put at just the right place." I understood this, but I had not made Liz understand it.

Punctuation marks are symbols, just as letters and words are (Angelillo, 2002), and they communicate messages to readers about how to read the written words. Grammar accomplishes this too—readers use grammar to make sense of the story (Weaver, 1996). Our oral speech is careless and filled with grammatical inaccuracies, but we have gestures, facial expressions, and voice inflection to help us express meaning. In writing, words stand alone. They need punctuation and grammar to shore them up, to communicate to readers how to read the words with intonation and inflection.

Some students think that punctuation and grammar are things to sprinkle on writing after they've finished, like adjusting the seasoning in soup. But good writers know that written conventions are essential ingredients for conveying meaning in writing.

So while students are composing, I urge you to avoid telling them, "Just write and forget about the punctuation and spelling." By encouraging them to ignore important conventions, we send a message that conventions really don't contribute to making meaning, and that they're something to add later. But unless they are writing in a particular genre (such as stream of consciousness, listing, or brainstorming), most writers write with correct punctuation and grammar. Conventions help them

## Plan a Punctuation Unit Early in the School Year

Carrying out a unit of study on punctuation inquiry in the fall does a great deal to help students discover why writers use punctuation. In my book *A Fresh Approach to Teaching Punctuation,* I detail how to do this. Students will come to understand the power and nuances of language. They will learn that proofreading for "mistakes" is different from composing with punctuation to shape meaning. While students must be careful and conscientious proofreaders, they must know how to compose using punctuation to convey meaning. Writing, composing, and thinking with punctuation are what good writers do.

shape meaning. So what we really should be saying to students is, "Don't let worrying about punctuation and grammar slow down or stop your thinking."

So what does this have to do with revision? When writers revise, they change words, rearrange chunks, rewrite to stay focused on one topic and in one genre. They also consider grammar—for example, they might think about verb tense and pronoun reference to help readers understand what is going on. They also consider punctuation—how it serves to clarify meaning and direct the reader. Care and respect for readers prompts writers to use conventions carefully and wisely. This thinking is vastly different from traditional thinking, which encourages us to dismiss grammar as stodgy nonsense or use punctuation as window-dressing. Punctuation is more than just periods and commas in the right places, and grammar is bigger than correct subject–verb agreement. They can be used to change and clarify meaning—and, ultimately, to create better writing. Putting a comma in the correct place is not as important as considering how that comma (or any mark, for that matter) will change or clarify meaning. For example, the placement of the comma in the title of Lynn Truss's book on punctuation, *Eats, Shoots and Leaves* (2004), makes all the difference between a panda eating a typical lunch of shoots and leaves, and a disgruntled diner eating lunch, shooting the waiter, and leaving with the police hot on his trail. Clearly the addition or elimination of a comma makes a difference, or as Pico Iyer tells us, makes us "hear a voice break, or a heart." In this chapter I look at ways to teach writers to revise using conventions. Specifically, I offer guidelines for

- studying punctuation in mentor sentences
- investigating how punctuation helps readers navigate long passages
- revising punctuation and grammar with meaning in mind

# STUDYING PUNCTUATION
# IN MENTOR SENTENCES

When I met with the fourth-grade teachers at Murray Avenue School in Mamaroneck, New York, they wanted to work on teaching students to write longer and more complex sentences as a way to improve writing. We discussed the ways we had been taught to write complex sentences when we went to school—through drill-and-kill exercises.

One of the teachers, Tina Dolan, shook her head. "I know my students," she said. "They are so bright and capable, but a lesson on dependent clauses or the function of commas will not excite them about writing. Let's think of another way."

Tina was so right. Her fourth graders did not need complicated rules of grammar to write longer sentences, no more than they needed to know the rules of physics to ride a bike. At some point, they would be ready for both the grammar and the physics lessons, but what they needed now was careful teaching using lots of high-quality examples.

For demonstration purposes, we chose a sentence from Cynthia Rylant's *The Cookie-Store Cat* (1999), a book the students knew well: "And now, after so many years, the bakers cannot remember ever being without a cookie-store cat." I displayed the sentence on the overhead and asked students to listen to my voice as I read it to them several times. Then I asked them to tell me any thoughts they had about the way I read it. Students had lots to say:

"It sounds like you're reading it slowly to stretch it out."

"The author was adding in some information between those commas."

"Makes me think of the way my grandmother talks, you know, after all these years."

"It would be hard to read that sentence if you didn't know when to move your voice around and when to slow down and speed up."

I asked students to read the sentence themselves with a partner. Tina and I walked around, listened to them, and heard them talk about how they liked the rhythm of the sentence once they knew how it should sound. They determined that punctuation helped Rylant shape the sentence so that her personality as a writer could come through. That excited them because they realized that punctuation could be used a guide, not an ironclad set of rules.

Following this partner work, the whole class talked about what it learned from this sentence. All students felt that it was a good model of how "extra information" (e.g., appositives: "after so many years") can be embedded into a sentence by using punctuation, which was something they were trying to do in their nonfiction writing.

From there, Tina and I let the students try writing sentences of their own, using Rylant's sentence structure as a model. First, we asked them to rewrite the sentence substituting only one word. Here's an example of what one student wrote:

## A Procedure for Studying Punctuation in Mentor Sentences

- Choose a high-quality sentence that has an interesting construction. You might look to children's books, magazines for young people, or your own writing. Put the sentence on a transparency and read it aloud to the class several times. Ask students to practice reading it aloud with a partner.

  > ORIGINAL RYLANT SENTENCE: "And now, after all these years, the bakers cannot remember ever being without a cookie-store cat."

- Ask partners to talk about what the sentence's punctuation accomplishes for them as readers.

- Continue reading aloud the sentence, changing one word each time. Be sure to maintain the sentences' structure and punctuation.

  > STAGE #1: "And now, after all these years, the Angelillo family cannot remember ever being without a cookie store cat." (changing one word)

  > STAGE #2: "And now, after all these years, the Angelillo family cannot remember ever being without a big black dog." (changing two words)

  > STAGE #3: "And finally, after all the messes, the Angelillo family cannot remember ever being without a big black dog." (changing three words)

- Ask students to try this on their own, using the same original sentence.

- Ask students to revisit drafts or notebook entries and find places where they could use the original sentence's structure and punctuation.

- Repeat the activity on subsequent days using different sentences and asking students to revise a draft or notebook entry each time for practice. By asking students to do this, you give the activity purpose.

- Ask students to find sentences on their own to practice on and use in revising their work.

"And now, after all these *minutes*, the cookie-store cat..." Then, we had the other students share their sentences. They were so delighted with the results, they asked if they could substitute more words. So we let them continue revising. Having read this sentence aloud so many times, they found the rhythm simple, and the punctuation seemed natural to them. Finally, we invited them to substitute all the words, while keeping Rylant's original structure. Harry R. Noden (1999) calls this imitating without plagiarizing. Here are some of the sentences students wrote:

> Last summer, with every one of my friends, I went to the Yankee game.

And now, after so many years, I still don't know how to swim.

Later on, when school is over, I'll go to the arcade.

And later, after I feed the dog, I'm going to go for a walk with her.

After school, when I changed my shoes, my friends and I played baseball in the park.

During lunch, after I eat, I'll go get an ice cream sundae with whipped cream and extra chocolate.

In class, before study hall, I'll go get my books.

Last Christmas, of all my family and friends, I got the most gifts of all.

Of course, our intention was not for students to write a sentence like Rylant's in every piece from then on. It was for students to understand that one way to learn to write complex sentences is to model your sentences on those a mentor author has written. We gave the students ways to study complex sentence structures through authors they knew, and ways to put those structures into their own writing.

# INVESTIGATING HOW PUNCTUATION HELPS READERS NAVIGATE LONG PASSAGES

Sarah Daunis's fifth-grade students in New York City became fascinated with punctuation when she did an initial unit on writing from a mentor sentence. So Sarah carried out a second unit that would help her students understand that punctuation is essential for readers to navigate through lots of print. She asked students to examine passages from mentor texts for ways that authors use punctuation to move readers along. The class chose several texts, including *Stones in Water* by Donna Jo Napoli and *Riding Freedom* by Pam Muñoz Ryan.

Sarah's students read the text passages, shared their findings with partners, and talked about ways to try out the punctuation in their own writing. Noticing what the writers did was helpful to them, but they also wanted to know "the rules." This was a good sign: They were progressing beyond the inquiry stage to learn the formal names of what they had noticed.

The students found that commas were particularly useful for guiding readers through long passages. So they decided to study commas in depth. Sarah supported them by providing books about writing that contain "rules" about comma use. (See box at right.) She also had copies of several children's books in which she had marked pages where long passages were punctuated using rules she wanted them to know. Most of the class decided that commas are essential to helping readers navigate long passages, but so are other punctuation marks, including colons, semicolons, and parentheses. Although students found that these marks are used more sparsely than commas, they still help readers navigate the meaning of the texts.

## Texts for Researching Punctuation Rules

*Punctuation Plain and Simple* by Edgar C. and Jean A. Alward, Career Press

*Grammatically Correct* by Ann Stilman, Writer's Digest Books

*The Elements of Style*, Fourth Edition, by William Strunk and E. B. White, Pearson Higher Education

*Punctuation Power* by Martin Terban, Scholastic

*Checking Your Grammar* by Martin Terban, Scholastic

*Write Right!*, Third Edition, by Jan Venolia, Ten Speed Press

# REVISING PUNCTUATION AND GRAMMAR WITH MEANING IN MIND

The cornerstone of many teachers' instructional practice is Louise Rosenblatt's transactional theory of reading. Rosenblatt (1994) wrote that literature has meaning only when a reader *makes meaning* from it. When we teach reading, we should teach students to transact with text to uncover the author's intended meaning, to react to the text, and to create meaning based on prior knowledge, experience, and familiarity with other texts.

When we teach writing, we too should consider Rosenblatt's theory. Young writers must acknowledge that readers will extract meaning from texts they create. In other words, reading is a transaction, or exchange of meaning, between readers and writers. Readers and writers have a reciprocal relationship. As writers, we have a responsibility to use whatever tools we can to help readers extract meaning that is as close to our intention as possible. Of course, readers may interpret a text according to their own thoughts or biases, but nonetheless writers should strive to make their meaning clear.

## A Procedure for Investigating How Punctuation Helps Readers Navigate Long Passages

- Be sure your students have done an initial inquiry into punctuation.

- Ask students to meet in partners to discuss ways they use punctuation in their writing.

- Locate several longer passages of writing where the authors use punctuation to aid the reader's ability to follow the message.

- Ask students to examine passages and name how the authors use punctuation.

- Encourage students to identify one punctuation mark in the passage to study in depth.

- Demonstrate making revisions based on the punctuation mark, using a piece of your own writing.

- Ask students to revise the punctuation in drafts or notebook entries, using the same strategies you and the author did.

So what are the implications for revision? The conventions of written language, including punctuation and grammar, are key tools for writers. Readers expect certain conventions to help them negotiate a text. For example, in spoken language, we often move from past tense to present tense as we tell a story ("Yesterday I went to the store for bread. But there isn't any on the shelf, so I say to the storekeeper…"). While this is not correct English, we all understand and accept it in conversation. Hand gestures, facial expressions, voice tone, and body language help us to communicate meaning in conversation.

However, in written texts, most readers would be confused, or would need to do some extra comprehension work, if the text switched tenses in the middle. Readers expect that writers will choose a tense and point of view and stay with it. It makes reading easier. Of course, there are times when writers deliberately do not follow these conventions, such as when they are trying to re-create spoken language or create an effect. When readers encounter intentional misuse of language in a published text, they know that a writer is playing with the conventions. Young writers might try this sometimes, but in general, it's best for them to stay with accepted conventions so they don't become confused.

Much has been written on ways to teach grammar in context (Noden, 1999; Weaver, 1996; Weaver, McNally, & Moerman, 2001), that is, embedding grammar instruction within reading and writing, rather than teaching it in isolation. I prefer teaching all components of reading and writing within the context of authentic texts. Whether you choose to teach grammar in context, in isolation, or in a fashion that combines the two methods, it is always wise to point students to mentor texts. When students do not know if they are "violating" a grammar rule, we can show them what writers do and do not do, and how jarring it is when a convention is ignored. Writers manipulate conventions to get our attention. When they want us to read smoothly, they often follow accepted conventions. With this in mind, teacher Anouk Weiss designs a study on using punctuation and grammar to convey meaning for her third graders at PS 6 in Manhattan. She wants them to understand that conventions are so important to conveying meaning that no serious writer ignores them. Her class completed a mentor author study earlier in the year, as well as a study of punctuation, so now Anouk challenges them to combine what they learned in the studies. She asks them to study their mentor authors to expand what they already know about punctuation and to discover some new points about grammar. That is, she sends them back into texts they know well and asks them to

- reread a mentor text once to refresh their minds on what they already know about it

- reread it again and write on sticky notes anything new or different they see, especially with regard to punctuation

- talk with their partners about what they are thinking

- draw conclusions about how the author uses punctuation most of the time

At first Anouk's students feel that they have studied their texts enough and have little more to learn from them. But as they look closer, they find subtleties that interest them. They point to places where their authors "follow the rules," rather than bending or breaking them, and where the punctuation does what they call its "quiet work" of helping the reader understand. (See Figure 9-1 and Appendix D for a reproducible version of this chart). The students conclude that writers bend or stretch rules only if they want you to pay attention for some reason. Otherwise, they write within the conventions. Therefore, it's safer to follow the rules, unless you have a good reason for ignoring them.

The students also recognized that reading is easier with dependable conventions, such as periods at the end of sentences. Following conventions makes reading

| Mentor Author | Rule He or She Followed | Example from Text |
|---|---|---|
| Mem Fox | Using commas to separate sections of a sentence where she wants us to pause. | Possum Magic: The next morning, just before breakfast, she shouted,.... |
| John J. Muth | Using capital letters at beginnings of sentences, and periods at the end. | The Three Questions: Nikolai thought for a moment. Then he asked his second question. |
| Jacqueline Woodson | Using quotation marks to tell us how to read dialogue. | The Other Side: "Don't stare," my mama said. "It's not polite." |
| Barbara Cooney | Using semicolons to connect short sentences without connecting words. | Miss Rumphius: From the porch of her new house Miss Rumphius watched the sun come up; she watched it cross the heavens and sparkle on the water; and she saw it set in glory in the evening. |
| Charlotte Zolotow | Using a comma and a connecting word to join two short sentences. | The Seashore Book: We climb to the top of the dune, away from the ocean, but we stop and look down to the sea grass across the sea. |
| Tomie de Paola | Using commas after each item in a list. | The Clown of God: He would put on a clown's face, step out from the curtain before the play began, bow, open up a colorful bag, roll out a carpet, and begin. |
| Byrd Baylor | Using parentheses to add in extra information. | The Other Way to Listen: (I never said a word while he was listening.) |

FIGURE 9-1

Mentor authors who "follow the rules."

more predictable and therefore less difficult in many ways. Students decide that they are glad they know ways to stretch the rules for craft purposes, but they are just as glad they know how to apply the rules in expected ways. They also are happy to know that whenever they have a punctuation or grammar question, they can always look in one or more mentor texts for answers.

# Summary

We can teach students to write more complex sentences by teaching them to study mentor sentences. Once students have examined the structures and the rhythms of long sentences by skilled writers, they can begin applying those structures and rhythms in their own writing. Careful study on the sentence level helps students strengthen their writing muscles. Since revision often requires writers to reevaluate grammar and punctuation decisions they've made, young writers must learn this deliberate work. We must not mislead students by encouraging them to think that punctuation and grammar are stodgy concepts, only to be considered at the proofreading stage.

## Some Points to Remember

- Students must be taught to respect and even love written conventions.
- Teach punctuation and/or grammar in separate units of study. Treat them as important revision tools, not as stepchildren of the writing process.
- Show students how mentor authors use conventions to convey meaning; make a chart about what they discover, such as the one in Figure 9-1. Use the chart as the basis for lessons on using conventions to convey meaning.
- Model how to study the rhythm and structure of a sentence as a way to write longer sentences; do the same with longer passages.
- Give students time to practice and play with punctuation in notebooks and in drafts.
- Ask students to notice the punctuation and grammar in books they are reading and to talk about them with you in conferences and small groups.
- Teach mini-studies on specific areas of punctuation or grammar usage, such as ways to punctuate dialogue or ways to write in the past tense.

# CHAPTER TEN

# ASSESSING REVISION IN STUDENT WRITING

C ontinuous, thoughtful assessment of student performance—and of our teaching—is the backbone of good instruction. We cannot plan wisely unless and until we assess what our students know, what they need to know, and how effectively we are teaching them. We can teach well only to the extent that we know our students well. Tailoring instruction to students' needs is the only way to teach effectively; that tailoring begins with dependable and ongoing assessment. But considering how broad instruction is, how can we assess one small part of it called the writing process—and an even smaller part of that called revision?

Revision should not be set apart from the writing process. It must be assessed *within* the writing work that we expect students to do. We should build revision into the rubrics we design, and we should tell students our expectations for revision. We should assess how they are using strategies, the effectiveness of their revisions, and, most of all, the thought processes behind their revision decisions.

Since it's important to teach students the small things about revision as well as the large things, we should assess how they use simple strategies to improve their writing, and also observe them carefully to determine how they are changing the ways they live as revisers. In this chapter I present ideas for examining student progress in revision. Specifically, I address how to assess students'

- willingness to revise and their understanding of revision's purposes
- growth in automaticity, care, and thoughtfulness in using revision strategies
- dedicated and wise use of mentor texts

# ASSESSING STUDENTS' WILLINGNESS TO REVISE AND THEIR UNDERSTANDING OF REVISION'S PURPOSES

As much as we might expect some students to resist revision at the beginning of the year, we can also expect a good deal of that resistance to melt away as the year goes on. If we cover revision in each unit of study that we carry out, and we are explicit in our teaching, students should have many revision strategies at their fingertips and *should be using them*. Revision should not be a chore for students, nor should we have to cajole students once they have a foothold on how to use strategies. They know it is valuable and expected. Revision is what writers do, and it is not negotiable.

Therefore, it is important to assess student attitudes toward revision based on your observation, information you gather in conferences, and their writing products. Be sure to inform students that their attitudes toward revision are part of what you will assess. This does not mean the extent to which they smile or grumble about revision, but rather the extent to which they know how to revise, can revise without prodding from you, and can reflect on what they have done.

Reflecting on their revision processes should be part of all assessments. (See Figure 10-1.) You can ask students to write a short paragraph at the end of each

I go back to reread every sentence. I do it because it buys me time to think about the next sentence I have to write.
—Mariah, grade 6

When I revise, I go back and reread for one thing at a time. I can't do a lot of revisions on one piece because I get sick of it.
—Freida, grade 5

On my own, I only revise for voice. I like my writing to sound like it just came out of my mouth. But I revise for other things if the teacher makes me or if she gives me a checklist.
—Jorge, grade 6

I like to keep at my beginnings until they are good. I like to put in talking.
—Billy, grade 4

I hate to revise. I only do it because it makes my writing better. I revise when I can do things like Kevin Henkes because he's my mentor author.
—Anna, grade 5

It's good that I have to revise because I don't worry so much about what I write. I think I will revise on my own now that I know a lot about what to do.
—Jeff, grade 4

FIGURE 10-1

*Students reflect on their revision process at the end of a unit of study.*

unit of study reflecting on what they've learned as writers and how they've grown as revisers. Ask them to point out a new revision strategy they tried or a mentor author they used and to evaluate how it worked in their writing. Vicki Spandel (2001) tells us that what writers can assess they can revise. It is as crucial that students learn to assess themselves as it is that we assess them. Teaching becomes powerful when we use our observations and student reflections to plan instruction.

## Using Rubrics to Assess Revision

If you teach revision in each unit of study, be sure to assess revision in each unit, too. Many teachers use rubrics to do this. On the rubric, you might include steps of the writing process and revision strategies you have taught, including strategies from previous units so that the rubric is cumulative. At some point, revise the rubric itself to include only the most important or recent strategies, with space for you to write in others you notice the student using. You might ask students to indicate on their drafts where they used revision strategies from previous units as well as the strategies from the current unit. It is also important to assess whether students are moving toward automaticity—that is, assessing their own writing and revising it appropriately and independently. See Figures 2-1, 10-3, and 10-6, and Appendix E for sample rubrics.

Rubrics become just more pieces of paper to clutter writing folders unless we reflect on them and talk about them. The data we gather must be part of ongoing conversations about writing growth. Tell students what is on the rubric before they write, and when you add items to it. They should have access to blank rubrics as they revise so they can verify what's expected from them.

You might even ask students to assess themselves by reading through their writing, filling out a rubric, and handing it in with the final draft to get a sense of how they view their development. Remember that assessment should help writers figure out what to revise (Spandel, 2001), so it's important to teach children to be independent assessors.

## Conferring to Assess Revision

Conferring with students is just as important as evaluating them using rubrics. In conferences, you teach students new revision techniques, coach them on how to accomplish revisions, or discuss their finished work, focusing on their revision decisions. In assessment conferences, you look at students' work while they explain their revision thinking. Ask them questions about why they made certain decisions and find out which mentor texts helped them. You are less interested in whether the revisions actually worked—though obviously that is the ultimate goal—than in how the students' thinking as revisers is progressing. How they are using the strategies you taught, using mentor authors, and growing as independent revisers is your assessment goal.

## Dealing With Grades

While we are required to give grades on student work, grades are counterproductive. Nevertheless, giving grades is a "non-negotiable" for the vast majority of us, as distressing as that may be. If we believe that teaching will change the way students write and the way they live their lives, grading seems a petty and unworthy way to let them know how they're doing. It's like a minister, priest, imam, or rabbi rating us on spirituality. Barry Lane, author of *After the End*, writes, "Grades, like success, promote ambition, not education." When students write for a grade, they are doing it for us, their teachers, not for themselves. In place of grades, Lane suggests that we respond to student writing by writing back with honest questions, comments, and concerns. Honest reflection about what the writer has done well and practical suggestions for future work are much more helpful than grades. If you must give grades, let students know that they are the least significant part of your evaluation.

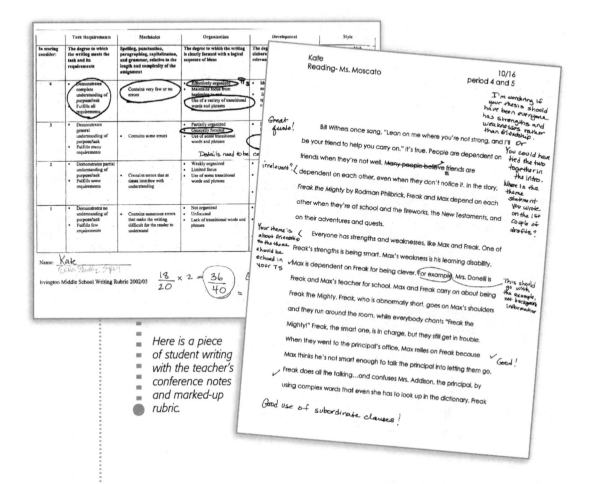

- Here is a piece
- of student writing
- with the teacher's
- conference notes
- and marked-up
- rubric.

Sometimes you will develop a "theory" about a student's learning that will inform what you cover in conferences. For example, you may realize that a student consistently has trouble elaborating on her writing, or maintaining a controlling focus. If that's the case, target these areas by teaching strategies that the student can apply at drafting and revising stages.

Karen Perepeluk and Maria Iams, fourth-grade teachers at PS 59 in Manhattan, focus on revision in every unit of study across the year. At the end of the year, they design a major assessment tool to reflect the hard work the class has done and to communicate to students the value they place on revision as part of the writing process. This assessment consists of teacher observations of revision behaviors during the revision unit of study, careful study of student work samples chosen by students for that purpose, written reflections by students, and end-of-year conferences.

FIGURE 10-2

# Interview Prompts for Assessing Revision in One Piece of Writing

- Tell me about your process for revising your writing work in this piece.

- Tell me about one revision decision you made and why you made it.

- Show me one place where you revised using the "advice" of your mentor author.

- Show me one place where you tried a revision strategy and it didn't work. Talk about why it failed you.

- Show me the most successful revision in this piece. What makes it successful?

- If you had time to do more revision, what would you do?

- What do you think you still need to learn about revision?

- What do you think about revision as a learner and a writer?

During end-of-year conferences, they ask students about the extent to which they have internalized revision strategies and behaviors, using a set of interview prompts. (See Figure 10-2.) Their goal is not to measure everything students have learned about writing but to evaluate thought processes around revision. In order to help students understand that they are responsible for revision all year, they ask them to point out revision strategies from previous units in their current writing. (See Figure 10-3.)

It's late in the school year, and Amy Condit, a sixth-grade teacher at Irvington Middle School, has given her students a good deal of direct instruction in revision. Since she values revision skills so highly, she tells students that their assessment will be based on what they point out as their most thoughtful and successful revisions in a completed piece of their choice. Each student highlights at least four revisions and then, in the margin or on an attached sheet, writes the thinking behind his or her decisions. Then Amy asks students to write a paragraph on at least one *major* revision they did, citing a mentor author they used, explaining why they chose to make the revision, and determining whether the revision is effective. The students also explain what they would try if they had to revise the piece again, and the types of revision they need to work on. This assessment encourages thorough reflection on the revision process and helps students plan for future revisions.

I have read over my work at least twice. One thing I noticed as I reread was:

I made the following major revision (highlight in orange on paper) because:

I revised one part (highlight in yellow) based on what I learned from my mentor author, _____

I used the following strategies from previous units. Write corresponding numbers on draft.

1. _____
2. _____
3. _____
4. _____

If I had more time, another revision I would make is:

**FIGURE 10-3**

*Here is a section of a rubric for assessing cumulative work in revision.*

Kerry Moscato teaches sixth grade at the same school. It's close to the end of the year, and Kerry feels most of her students have deepened their revision knowledge tremendously. Nevertheless, she wants to underscore the idea of using mentor authors, so she asks each student to reflect on how their writing and revising are influenced by those authors. She gives students their folders containing all their writing for the year, and asks them to look at each piece with these questions in mind:

- What is one huge change you see in your writing, especially in your revision work?

- How has your image of yourself as a reviser changed this year?

- What is the one most important thing you learned from your mentor author?

- What do you think you need to work on in the future as a reviser?

- Name a writer you think you might use as a mentor in the future.

Kerry expects that this work will help students realize that revising is an ongoing process, and that they can continue studying mentor authors. When we look at her students' reflections we see that they are thoughtful and reflective about themselves as revisers. This is due in large part to Kerry's good teaching.

We are responsible for doing whatever we can to make the revision habit "stick." When we create conditions for students to see that a skill is something they need and can use, they are more likely to master it (Cambourne, 1991). Asking students to reflect on themselves as revisers encourages them to view revision as worth doing in life.

# Assessing Students' Growth in Automaticity, Care, and Thoughtfulness in Using Revision Strategies

It is important to assess how automatically, carefully, and thoughtfully students use revision strategies. I am less interested in having students produce perfect writing than I am in having certain behaviors, such as revising automatically and thoughtfully when writing. We want to avoid having students looking at charts of revision strategies and then using each one without any thought to how or why they are doing so. Students need and deserve direct instruction to know how and when to use the strategies, as well as lots of practice. Practice should make revision second

- Check spelling or circle to fix later.
- Try to write a good beginning before I write more.
- Imagine real people saying the dialogue I write.
- Highlight words I want to change.
- Put a box around a part I don't like and need to fix.
- Put a star next to a part that doesn't belong. Use an arrow to put it somewhere else.
- Cross out parts I don't want in light pencil.
- Use a caret to add a word in.
- Add sentence in the margin.

- Put question mark where something is not clear.
- Take a break when I get too tired.
- Read it out loud to myself.
- Read it to my partner or let my partner read it and tell me what I need.
- Look at my mentor author and find something I want to check in my writing.
- Put an "X" on a place I want to rewrite or play around with in my notebook.
- Put an "X" on a place that I have no idea what to do with – I have to ask someone.
- Think of mentor texts my writing sounds like and be proud of myself.

**FIGURE 10-4**

*A student lists revision strategies that he uses automatically.*

nature to them, giving them opportunities to make wise revision choices. Part of practicing is being allowed to make mistakes, an important part of learning.

Lisa Schofield, a fourth-grade teacher at Main Street School in Irvington, New York, worries that her revision teaching will not "stick" when her students have left her class, so she decides to look at students' revision behaviors. What do her students do *without* her prompting that indicates they've internalized the strategies she's taught them? She asks her students to write about revisions they make in their notebooks, *as they are composing,* as well as revisions they make when they revisit the writing. Her aim is to teach students to "watch themselves" as they write, so that they notice the revision strategies that they use automatically. Lisa hopes they will continue to add to their notebooks as they learn more about themselves. (See Figure 10-4.)

This exercise shows Lisa not only the students who are using strategies as they compose and after they compose, but also those who aren't. When this happens, she pulls together a guided writing group (Fountas & Pinnell, 2001) of students who are not using strategies to help them. From there, she encourages them to list things they could do to revise "on the fly." The students list strategies they feel they could use while working on first drafts, as well as things they could do in later revision. (See Figure 10-5 and Appendix D for a reproducible version of this chart.) Over time, students begin to understand that writers revise as they write, and that they should work toward some automatic revision in their writing.

| What I Will Revise Immediately | What I Will Revise Later |
| --- | --- |
| Making characters clear | Dialogue for each character |
| Being sure there is setting | Adding in extra setting details |
| Making the problem really important | Adding in character's thinking about it |
| Knowing what the end will be | Writing the end when we are not tired |

FIGURE 10-5

*A student decides what to revise immediately and what to revise later.*

Lisa's main purpose is to assess the degree to which her students revise deliberately and automatically. She wants her students to know that revising is not random and that a writer does not use every strategy every time he or she writes.

# Assessing Students' Dedicated and Wise Use of Mentor Texts

As teachers, we want our students to become independent. But for that to happen, we must give them the means. As I discussed in Chapter 3, knowing how to use mentor texts is crucial to learning because it enables students to direct their own work. Effective writing-workshop teaching will focus on using a selection of mentor texts for whole-class work and will also steer students toward their own mentor texts and support their independent use of them.

Judy Nadler, a fifth-grade teacher in Irvington, New York, does that by adding a "mentor texts" section to the rubrics she uses in all her units of study. The section gives her the security of knowing that her students are using mentor

## The "Mentor Text" Section of a Writing Rubric

FIGURE 10-6

| STRATEGY: | SECURE | DEVELOPING | BEGINNING | TEACHER'S COMMENTS |
|---|---|---|---|---|
| Use of mentor text for guidance in revision: | Student makes use of mentor text by relying on it for revision strategies and using those strategies in his or her own writing; sophistication in revision or text choice is apparent | Student makes some revisions based on mentor text, but rationale for choosing revisions is not clear; some choices appear to be random or not well thought out. | Student makes few or no revisions based on learning from the mentor text.<br><br>Student is unclear about the value of using mentor texts. | *Blank section for teacher to give advice or note insightful work.* |

Write a short paragraph about how you used your mentor text to revise your writing in this piece. Be as detailed as you can. (5 points)

texts independently before she sends them off to middle school. All year long, Judy asks students to name the authors and texts they use and how they help them. In addition, her rubric explicitly states levels of expertise in using the texts. (See Figure 10-6.) Judy wants her students to understand that knowing how to use mentor texts will serve them well in middle school. And to help them further, she has students make a list of authors of mentor texts that they might need. (See Figure 10-7.) Her students know they can continue to learn from the authors they've studied, but that there is also much to learn from other authors.

Use of a mentor text shouldn't be limited to making craft decisions or finding ideas for organization. Be sure that your class knows that a mentor text can inspire ideas for topics, voice, and style, and formats for telling a story, such as

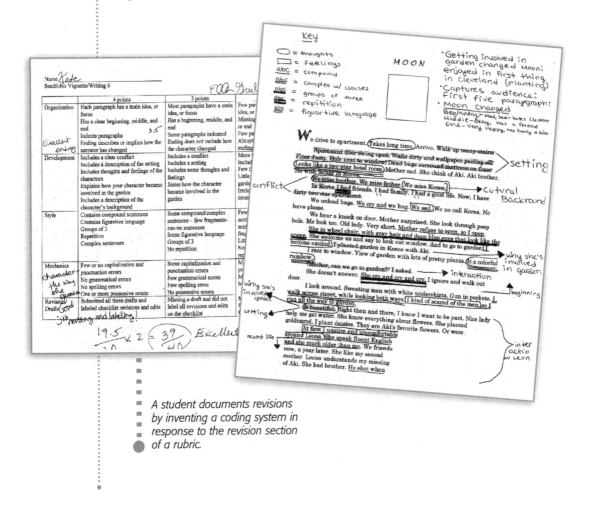

*A student documents revisions by inventing a coding system in response to the revision section of a rubric.*

first-person narrative, journal entries, flashbacks, and so on. Also be sure that your class understands that it can learn something from every writer. For every text in the library, there is something they can teach themselves about writing.

# SUMMARY

Revision should be only one part of your overall, ongoing writing assessment program. That said, we can learn a great deal about students' thinking by focusing on their revision process—on the mind work that went into their revision decisions. Assess the quality of students' revisions, but turn a closer eye to what the process of making those revisions tells us about how students think and learn. Designing rubrics that reflect what you consider important about revision, and including sections on mentor texts, will bring you one step closer to that goal.

Ultimately, assessment makes us look at ourselves and our teaching. We must think about ways to make our teaching precise, clear, and long-lasting. For our students to grow as revisers, we must grow as teachers.

## Some Points to Remember

- Assessing students' products is only one part of the assessment picture.

- Assessing their process is important, too.

- Don't rely on rubrics too heavily. They should be one tool to use along with observations and conferences.

- Ask students to talk and write about their revision processes, as well as the specific decisions they made when they revised.

- Encourage students to refer to mentor authors and texts as ways to build independence.

- Always use assessment results to plan future teaching and learning.

**FIGURE 10-7**

**Mentor Authors Appropriate for Middle School**

Laurie Halse Anderson

Robert Cormier

Paula Fox

Carl Hiaasen

Walter Dean Myers

Donna Jo Napoli

Richard Peck

Mildred Taylor

# THE MOST DELICIOUS PART

**A**ll the revision strategies in the world, all the charts on walls and rubrics in folders, mean little if revision does not take hold of children's lives. Revision is more than a way to make writing better. It is a way to live a thoughtful, robust life. It's a way to enjoy our talents and successes, and grow closer to our vision of ourselves. Revision enables us to live and think as problem solvers. It's why we diet—we want to improve our health or our looks. It's why we save money—we want to live on a little farm someday. It's why we have families— we want to have people to love for a long time. All of that is revision, looking at what we are, what we've done, what we have, and making it who we are. That is what we teach students when we teach them to revise.

And writing? Yes, we have to revise that, too.

Most writers want to revise. They know that writing is revising. As Michael Crichton says, "Books aren't written. They are rewritten." Toni Morrison likes to get that first draft down, because she knows she can go back again and again. For her, the "most delicious part" is revising.

I believe most students avoid revision because they don't know how to do it. They don't know how to look at a draft, find what works and praise themselves, and find what doesn't work and fix it. They're a lot more likely to notice something "broken" if they have tools. Students must practice revising writing like violinists and soccer players practice—they practice hard, to the point where the effort no longer shows and it looks like their work is flawless. The writer's aim is to get so good at revision that it no longer shows—the writing appears perfect, and the reader doesn't see that the writer has "just opened a vein" (Brohaugh, 1987).

Students who don't know how to revise or who refuse to revise miss some of the very best thinking they can do. They haven't been shown how to revise by studying authors. They haven't been given the time and permission to play as revisers. And chances are, they do not have teachers who are themselves revisers. I can be honest with students because I've struggled with revising, so I know how it feels. As teachers, we must know what it's like to study a page of Barbara Kingsolver and wonder, "How does she do that?" And we must know the satisfying joy of solving a problem by thinking long and hard about it. Until teachers revise their own writing, our pleas for revision will fall on deaf ears. We cannot speak with authority. It's as if I tried to "teach" you to play golf by telling you all the things you should do, but never holding a golf club myself. Silly, isn't it? Yet it happens all the time in writing classrooms.

Go write. Go read. Go study some writers. Do it for your students, but most of all, do it for yourself. Revise your writing. Revise your teaching. Revise your life.

# Appendix A
## Supporting the Teaching of Revision: What Administrators and Coaches Can Do

- Set aside time for teachers to meet and revise their curriculum calendars to include revision in every unit of study. Ask them to consider revision within and across grades.

- Ask teachers to devote at least one unit of study exclusively to revision, in addition to an author study.

- Use faculty meetings as a time to study student work and plan revision instruction.

- Set aside time for teachers to meet in study groups on writing and revision. They might discuss topics such as teaching students to use mentor authors, overcoming student resistance, and using assessment results to plan instruction.

- Consider establishing a school-wide revision project as a year-end assessment.

- Go into classrooms to read high-quality books aloud and think aloud about revision.

- Do your own writing and share your revisions with students.

- Meet with teachers to study student writing on a regular basis. Read their conferring notes and instructional plans for individual students.

- Observe teachers during revision lessons and schedule pre- and post-observation conferences with them to support practice related to revision.

- Establish a committee or study group to read children's literature and recommend new books for use in revision lessons.

- Ask teachers to establish benchmarks for the level of revision they expect to see in each grade.

- Ask the media specialist to establish a filing system for students' published pieces and drafts of those pieces, so they can be easily accessed for teaching purposes.

- Be sure classrooms have rich libraries that contain nonfiction and fiction.

- Talk with teachers about the importance of using revision strategies in content-area work throughout the day.

- Coach and confer with students, help them find mentor texts, coteach lessons using your own writing, and help teachers plan.

# Becoming a Teacher Leader in Your School

Teacher leaders are essential to school change. Without key people who are willing and able to act as resources, change tends to lose momentum and sputter to a halt. While some colleagues may resist change, teacher leaders show by example how change can work. They lead others to a place where their natural talent and wisdom can shine. They carry the message that change is inevitable, not just in schools, but in everything we do in life. With dedication and wisdom, teacher leaders can support change so that it becomes part of the school culture and community. Here are some things you can do as a teacher leader:

- Invite others into you classroom on a regular basis. Rather than ask them to "observe" you, ask them to help you study one aspect of your teaching. So, for example, you might invite someone to sit in on two conferences and then meet to talk with you later about them. Form partnerships with nonleaders and meet with them often.

- Form study groups about topics that interest you—such as revision—and that might interest other teachers. Schedule meetings at a convenient time. Keep them low-key and friendly, but stay on the topic. It helps to make the meeting schedule clear—for example, once a week for five weeks. People are more likely to commit to a group if they feel they are not giving up their entire semester or year. (See Appendix C.) Send out invitations and/or post an announcement in the teachers' room or office, and follow up by e-mailing people or reminding them in person. Take suggestions from teachers about topics they might be interested in and plan future study groups accordingly. That way, if they won't commit today, they might later on.

- Form a book discussion group about a piece of professional literature, a piece of children's literature, or both. I find that teachers like to meet to get ideas about how to use specific books in their teaching.

- Be able to point group members to professional resources that can help them. Over time, you will know many books to recommend to others—and you will become a better teacher for it. Get ideas from other leaders and possibly meet to "report" on books that only one or two of you have had the time to read.

- Plan regular meetings with other teacher leaders and talk together about ways to handle common problems.

- Offer to visit other teachers to help them with their teaching—but be sure to focus on only one aspect, such as rethinking the classroom environment to support instruction or making mini-lessons shorter but more effective.

- Meet regularly with the principal and/or assistant principal to discuss how things are going. Because administrators enter classrooms in a different capacity than yours, they can advise you on which teachers would benefit most from your help. And you can advise them on who needs a pat on the back, who needs more books in her library, and so on.

- Go to local and national professional conferences such as NCTE and IRA. Write grants or ask district personnel to help you with costs.

- Focus on helping teachers to solve problems, rather than expecting them to be experts. Problems are opportunities for learning. Therefore, if a teacher is concerned that his students are not revising, that teacher should study revision. And if you find the same problem happening in one another's rooms, you can research and figure it out together.

## Appendix C
# Organizing Study Groups Around Revision

Even without a staff developer, you can meet with colleagues to expand your knowledge on any topic that interests you. You may begin as the organizer of the group and then let others take the reins, with a different teacher leading each meeting. All you need is a commitment of time and a few inquiring minds. Here are some general ideas for forming a five-week cycle of study, focused on teaching revision:

- Identify one aspect of revision that you would like to study, such as assessing student work and planning instruction, using mentor texts, or teaching revision of a particular genre.

- Plan five meetings and ask an administrator for support, perhaps by providing a room to meet, purchasing books to study, or participating as a member of the group. Ask interested colleagues to commit to all meetings. Early mornings or late afternoons are usually best. Rob Ross and Marilyn Lopez's Tuesday breakfast meetings at PS 206 in Queens, New York, became an institution—satellite groups formed when too many teachers wanted to participate.

- Create a plan for each week and keep to it. For example, before the first meeting, teachers might read a short section of this book and come ready to discuss it.

- Be sure that teachers try out ideas in their classes and report back to the group, using student work to illustrate their points.

- Take minutes at each meeting and prepare a short memo after the last meeting to summarize the group's work. Share the memo with all participants and administrators.

# A Five-Week Plan for Three Study Groups on Revision

| | Reading and Discussing Professional Literature to Study Revision | Reading Student Writing for Revision Ideas | Using Children's Literature to Teach Revision |
|---|---|---|---|
| Week #1 | Teachers read a portion of *Making Revision Matter* beforehand, and come prepared to discuss or respond to it. For the next meeting, they agree to read another selection on teaching revision. Consider books by authors such as Fletcher, Davis and Hill, Ray, Lane, and Heard. (See "Professional References Cited" for details.) | Each teacher chooses three students and studies his or her work and progress over five weeks. To the first meeting, she brings samples of the students' work. She discusses the students' strengths and the revision strategy that is most important to teach each student. | The lead teacher brings a short mentor text he or she has used for teaching revision and demonstrates how she's taught revision strategies using it. At the end of the meeting, another teacher agrees to bring a text to think about next time. |
| Week #2 | Teachers bring lessons or student work related to selections they have read and discuss how professional literature is informing practice. Teachers self-assign more reading for next meeting. | Each teacher brings conferring notes and recent writing of the three students, and is ready to discuss how whole-class teaching and conferring is helping each student. Teachers help one another develop ideas on what to teach next. | Teachers discuss the short mentor text and revision strategies, and plan two revision lessons based on it. They choose new texts to share at the next meeting. |
| Week #3 | Teachers plan lessons together that reflect the professional reading, targeting topics that seem especially challenging. They discuss how to overcome obstacles, including issues related to time, student resistance, and gaps in their knowledge. | Teachers discuss changes and challenges they see in students' work, and plan small-group revision work based on those observations. | Teachers share their two lessons and discuss implications for teaching with the new texts they've brought. |
| Week #4 | Teachers focus on what is difficult for them to teach in revision, and discuss answers in the professional literature. | Teachers discuss their biggest challenges in teaching revision and brainstorm ways to overcome them, trying out ideas on drafts of their own writing. | Teachers plan out an author study together, which includes revision lessons. They brainstorm the content of lessons based on their assessments of their classes. |
| Week #5 | Teachers reflect on the power of reading professional literature regularly and make plans for further reading on their own or in pairs. | Teachers reflect on student progress from first meeting to last, making plans to continue the work by studying other students' writing. | Teachers share student revision work that grows out of literature study. They reflect and plan for further literature study. |

# Preparing for Story Writing by Playing with Notebook Ideas

**Name** _____ **Date** _____

| My Idea from My Notebook | Why It Won't Work | What If...? |
|---|---|---|
|  |  |  |
|  |  |  |
|  |  |  |

An explanation of how to use this reproducible form appears on page 84.

© Scholastic Inc. *Making Revision Matter.* page 194

# Revision Reflection

**Name** _____ **Date** _____

**One important revision I made was:** _____

_____

_____

_____

**I decided to make this revision because:** _____

_____

_____

_____

**One revision I am extra proud of is:** _____

_____

_____

_____

**I used my mentor author to revise this:** _____

_____

_____

_____

**A revising skill I want to learn is:** _____

_____

_____

_____

An explanation of how to use this reproducible form appears on page 152.

© Scholastic Inc. *Making Revision Matter* page 195

# Uncovering Recurring Revision Trends

**Name** _____ **Date** _____

| Revision Trend | Example from My Writing | My Revised Writing | Plan for My Future Writing |
|---|---|---|---|
| | | | |
| | | | |
| | | | |

An explanation of how to use this reproducible form appears on page 162.

© Scholastic Inc. *Making Revision Matter* page 196

# Identifying Mentor Authors Who "Follow the Rules"

**Name** _____  **Date** _____

| Mentor Author | Rule He or She Followed | Example from Text |
|---|---|---|
|  |  |  |
|  |  |  |
|  |  |  |
|  |  |  |
|  |  |  |
|  |  |  |

An explanation of how to use this reproducible form appears on page 174.

© Scholastic Inc. *Making Revision Matter* page 197

# Deciding What to Revise Immediately and What to Revise Later

**Name** _____ **Date** _____

| What I Will Revise Immediately | What I Will Revise Later |
|---|---|
| | |
| | |
| | |
| | |

# Rubric for Assessing Revision

**Name** _____ **Date** _____

**Revision Phase:**
• Mark at least three places in your draft where you did major revisions.
• Write in the margin of your draft why you decided to do them.
• Write the name of your mentor author and what you learned from him or her.
• Mark at least three places in your draft where you did minor revisions.
• Write in the margin of your draft why you decided to do them.

**Name one revision that makes you proud and why.**

**Name one new revision strategy you tried.**

**Which new revision strategy will you use again?**

## Appendix E

# Rubric for Assessing Realistic Fiction

| | 4 POINTS | 3 POINTS | 2 POINTS | 1 POINT |
|---|---|---|---|---|
| **ORGANIZATION** | • Each paragraph has a main idea, or focus<br>• Has a clear beginning, middle, and end<br>• Indents paragraphs<br>• Ending describes or implies how the narrator has changed | • Most paragraphs have a main idea or focus<br>• Has a beginning, middle, and end<br>• Some paragraphs indented<br>• Ending does not include how the character changed | • Few paragraphs have a main idea or focus<br>• Missing a beginning, middle, or end<br>• Few paragraphs indented<br>• Abrupt or undeveloped ending | • Paragraphs are unclear and no clear sequence is evident |
| **DEVELOPMENT** | • Includes clear conflict<br>• Includes a description of the setting<br>• Includes thoughts and feelings of the characters<br>• Explains how the character became involved in the situation<br>• Includes a description of the character's background | • Includes a conflict<br>• Includes a setting<br>• Includes some thoughts and feelings<br>• States how the character became involved in the situation | • More than one conflict<br>• Includes a setting<br>• Few thoughts and feelings<br>• Little connection to the situation<br>• Irrelevant or repetitive details | • No conflict evident<br>• Few thoughts and feelings<br>• Details are unclear, irrelevant, and/or repetitive |
| **STYLE** | • Contains compound sentences<br>• Contains figurative language<br>• Groups of three<br>• Repetition<br>• Complex sentences | • Some compound/complex sentences—few fragments and/or run-on sentences<br>• Some figurative language<br>• Groups of three<br>• No repetition | • Few compound/complex sentences—all simple sentences and/or some fragments or run-ons<br>• Little figurative language<br>• No groups of three or repetition | • Many fragments and/or run-on sentences<br>• No figurative language, groups of three, or repetition |
| **MECHANICS** | • Few or no capitalization and punctuation errors<br>• No grammatical errors<br>• No spelling errors<br>• One or more possessive nouns | • Some capitalization and punctuation errors<br>• Few grammatical errors<br>• Few spelling errors<br>• No possessive nouns | • Many capitalization and punctuation errors<br>• Many grammatical errors<br>• Many spelling errors | • Numerous errors that interfere with understanding |
| **REVISIONS/ DRAFTS** | • Submitted all three drafts and labeled checklist revisions and edits | • Missing a draft and did not label all revisions and edits on the checklist | • Missing a draft and labeled few revisions and edits on the checklist | • Missing drafts |

Source: Irvington Middle School, Irvington, NY

# Rubric for Assessing Realistic Fiction (alternate)

| | 4 POINTS: AWESOME | 3 POINTS: ADMIRABLE | 2 POINTS: ACCEPTABLE | 1 POINT: ATTEMPT |
|---|---|---|---|---|
| **ORGANIZATION** | • Structure has a beginning, middle, and end, or it is a series of moments connected by a theme<br>• Logical order<br>• Focused on the same subject<br>• Indents paragraphs | • Structure has a beginning, middle, and end, or it is a series of moments<br>• Most ideas are in a logical order<br>• Mostly focused<br>• Most paragraphs indented | • Part of the text lacks structure<br>• Some ideas are in a logical order<br>• Little focus<br>• Some paragraphs indented | • Story is unclear and incoherent<br>• No focus or structure evident |
| **DEVELOPMENT** | • Describes what people, places, and things look like<br>• Includes effective dialogue<br>• Includes thoughts of the narrator<br>• Setting is established<br>• Includes feelings of the narrator<br>• Ending is reflective/refers to the here and now | • Uses some descriptive language<br>• Includes thoughts of the narrator<br>• Setting is established<br>• Includes feelings of the narrator<br>• Ending is evident<br>• Ending refers to the here and now | • Uses little descriptive language<br>• Includes few thoughts of the narrator<br>• Setting is established<br>• Includes few feelings of the narrator<br>• Ending is not reflective and does not refer to here and now | • Uses no descriptive language<br>• Includes no thoughts of the narrator<br>• Setting is not established<br>• Includes no feelings of the narrator<br>• Ending is unclear or not evident |
| **STYLE** | • Complete complex sentences with subordinate clauses<br>• Simple and compound sentences<br>• Rich language | • Some complex sentences with subordinate clauses<br>• Some compound sentences<br>• Clear language | • Few complex sentences with subordinate clauses<br>• Mostly simple sentences<br>• Uses grade-appropriate language | • Attempts to use complex sentences<br>• Only simple sentences<br>• Uses simple language |
| **MECHANICS** | • Sentences contain few spelling, capitalization, and punctuation errors | • Sentences contain some capitalization, punctuation, and spelling mistakes | • Sentences contain many errors in capitalization, punctuation, and spelling | • Sentences contain too many errors in capitalization, punctuation, and spelling |

Source: Irvington Middle School, Irvington, NY

# Rubric for Assessing a Feature Article

| | 4 POINTS: MASTER | 3 POINTS: PROFICIENT | 2 POINTS: EMERGING | 1 POINT: NOVICE |
|---|---|---|---|---|
| **MEANING** | • The feature article has a main idea, or angle<br>• Angle is supported through the use of facts<br>• The angle, facts, and thinking are logical and communicated effectively | • Has a main idea, or angle<br>• Angle is supported with some facts<br>• Most facts and thinking are logical and connected to the angle | • Main idea, or angle, is a little unclear<br>• Some facts and thinking are logical and connected to the angle | • Main idea, or angle, is unclear<br>• Facts and thinking are illogical and not connected to the angle |
| **DEVELOPMENT** | • Ideas are developed with facts, statistics, and anecdotes<br>• New words are defined<br>• Irrelevant or unrelated details are omitted<br>• 3 subcategories or more support angle<br>• Reflective thinking is included | • Some ideas are developed with facts, statistics, and anecdotes<br>• Some new words are defined<br>• A few irrelevant or repetitive details<br>• 3 subcategories<br>• Some reflective thinking | • Few ideas are developed with facts, statistics, and anecdotes<br>• Few words are defined<br>• Irrelevant and repetitive details<br>• 3 subcategories<br>• Little reflective thinking | • Ideas are not developed with relevant facts, statistics, and anecdotes<br>• No words are defined<br>• Irrelevant and repetitive details<br>• No reflective thinking |
| **ORGANIZATION** | • Each paragraph has a main idea and topic sentence<br>• Introduction engages the reader and states the angle<br>• Sentences and subcategories follow a logical sequence of ideas<br>• Conclusion wraps up the feature article and connects to the angle | • Most paragraphs have main ideas and topic sentence<br>• Introduction states the angle<br>• Most sentences and subcategories are sequenced logically<br>• Conclusion connects to the angle | • Some paragraphs have main ideas and topic sentences<br>• Introduction is unclear<br>• Some sentences and subcategories are sequenced logically<br>• Conclusion is evident | • Few paragraphs have main ideas and topic sentences<br>• Introduction is unclear<br>• Information is not in a logical order<br>• No conclusion |
| **SENTENCE** | • Sentences are complete—no run-ons or fragments (unless discussed with me)<br>• Sentence beginnings vary<br>• Compound sentences and subordinate clauses<br>• Voice is not formal, but engaging and familiar | • Some incomplete or run-on sentences<br>• Some sentence variety<br>• Sentences are simple and compound<br>• Voice is engaging | • Many incomplete sentences and run-ons<br>• Little sentence variety<br>• Sentences are simple<br>• Little voice evident | • Numerous incomplete sentences or run-ons<br>• Simple sentences<br>• No voice |
| **MECHANICS** | • Few spelling, punctuation, and capitalization errors | • Some spelling, punctuation, and capitalization errors | • Many spelling, punctuation, and capitalization errors | • Too many errors to understand the text |
| **PRESEN-TATION** | • Typed, 1 or 2 graphics or quotes that stand out<br>• Neat and organized | • No graphics or quotes<br>• Neat | • No graphics or quotes<br>• Information is disorganized on the page | • Handwritten with no graphics or quotes<br>• Disorganized |

Source: Irvington Middle School, Irvington, NY

# One School's Curriculum Plan

## CURRICULUM PLAN FOR THIRD-GRADE WRITING WORKSHOP

| SEPTEMBER Unit 1 | OCTOBER Unit 2 | NOVEMBER Unit 3 | DECEMBER Unit 4 | JANUARY Unit 5 (first two weeks) | FEBRUARY Unit 6 (includes last two weeks of January) | MARCH Unit 7 | APRIL Unit 8 | MAY Unit 9 | JUNE Unit 10 |
|---|---|---|---|---|---|---|---|---|---|
| Assessment/ Testing | Launching | Craft (with a convention unit) Author Study Publish with two revisions | Personal Narrative | Narrative How to tell a good story–story elements State Test Prompts (Narrative) | Nonfiction: Feature Article | Poetry (can include a memoir poem) | Writing about Reading | Realistic Fiction | Revision Reflection Writing Projects |

## CURRICULUM PLAN FOR FOURTH-GRADE WRITING WORKSHOP

| SEPTEMBER Unit 1 | OCTOBER Unit 2 | NOVEMBER Unit 3 | DECEMBER Unit 4 | JANUARY Unit 5 | FEBRUARY Unit 6 | MARCH Unit 7 | APRIL Unit 8 | MAY Unit 9 | JUNE Unit 10 |
|---|---|---|---|---|---|---|---|---|---|
| Assessment State Test Prompts (Narrative) | Launching Short Publishing (until the end of first week of November) | Written Conventions and Revision | Poetry | Writing about Reading | Realistic Fiction | Speech-writing | Punctuation and Revision | Nonfiction: Report and Feature Article | Revision Reflection Writing Projects |

## CURRICULUM PLAN FOR FIFTH-GRADE WRITING WORKSHOP

| SEPTEMBER Unit 1 | OCTOBER Unit 2 | NOVEMBER Unit 3 | DECEMBER Unit 4 | JANUARY Unit 5 | FEBRUARY Unit 6 | MARCH Unit 7 | APRIL Unit 8 | MAY Unit 9 | JUNE Unit 10 |
|---|---|---|---|---|---|---|---|---|---|
| Test Prep Assessment | Launching 2-week convention unit | Personal Narrative | Expository Writing: Essay | Nonfiction: Editorial | Writing About Reading | Poetry Convention unit | Persuasive Essay | Historical Fiction | Revision Reflection |

Source: Julian Curtiss School, Greenwich, CT

# Professional References Cited

Allen, J. (1999). *Words, words, words: Teaching vocabulary in grades 4–12.* Portland, ME: Stenhouse.

Anderson, C. (2000). *How's it going? A practical guide to conferring with student writers.* Portsmouth, NH: Heinemann.

Anderson, C. (in press). *What do I teach today? Linking assessment and teaching in the writing workshop.* Portsmouth, NH: Heinemann.

Anderson, L. W., & Krathwohl, D. R. (Eds.) (2001). *A taxonomy for learning, teaching, and assessing: A revision of Bloom's taxonomy of educational objectives.* New York: Longman.

Angelillo, J. (2002). *A fresh approach to teaching punctuation.* New York: Scholastic.

Angelillo, J. (2003). *Writing about reading: From book talk to literary essays, grades 3–8.* Portsmouth, NH: Heinemann.

Bambara, T. C. (1980). What it is I think I'm doing anyhow. In J. Sternburg (Ed.), *The writer on her work.* New York: Norton.

Bannister, L. (1993). *Three women revise: What Morrison, Oates, and Tan can teach our students about revision.* Paper presented at the annual meeting of the Conference on College Composition and Communication. San Diego, CA.

Beck, I., McKeown, M. G., & Kucan, L. (2002). *Bringing words to life: Robust vocabulary instruction.* New York: Guilford Press.

Bickham, J. M. (1993). *Setting: How to create and sustain a sharp sense of time and place in your fiction.* Cincinnati, OH: Writer's Digest Books.

Bishop, W. (2004). *Acts of revision.* Portsmouth, NH: Heinemann.

Boiarsky, C. (1981). *The eleven functions of revision.* Paper presented at the annual meeting of the Conference on College Composition and Communication. Dallas, TX.

Brohaugh, W. (Ed.). (1987). *Just open a vein.* Cincinnati, OH: Writer's Digest Books.

Bruner, J. S. (1986). *Actual minds, possible worlds.* Cambridge, MA: Harvard University Press.

Calkins, L. M. (1983). *Lessons from a child.* Portsmouth, NH: Heinemann.

Calkins, L. M. (1986). *The art of teaching writing.* Portsmouth, NH: Heinemann.

Calkins, L. M. (1994). *The art of teaching writing, New ed.* Portsmouth, NH: Heinemann.

Calkins, L. M., et al. (2003). *Units of study in the primary workshop.* Portsmouth, NH: Heinemann.

Cambourne, B. (1991). *Coping with chaos.* Portsmouth, NH: Heinemann.

Chrenka, L., Balkema, S., Kuzma, F., & Vasicek, B. (1996). *Revision blocked: Assessing a writer's development.* Paper presented at the annual meeting of the Conference on College Composition and Communication. Milwaukee, WI.

Cruz, M. C. (2004). *Independent writing.* Portsmouth, NH: Heinemann.

Culham, R. (2003). *6 + 1 traits of writing: The complete guide, grades 3 and up.* New York: Scholastic.

Daiute, C. A. (1982). Psycholinguistic perspectives on revising. In R. A. Sudol (Ed.), *Revising: New essay for teachers of writing.* Urbana, IL: NCTE.

Davis, J., & Hill, S. (2003). *The no-nonsense guide to teaching writing.* Portsmouth, NH: Heinemann.

Dean, N. (2000). *Voice lessons: Classroom activities to teacher diction, detail, imagery, syntax, and tone.* Gainesville, FL: Maupin House.

Dibell, A. (1988). *Plot: How to build short stories and novels that don't sag, fizzle, or trail off in scraps of frustrated revision—and how to rescue stories that do.* Cincinnati, OH: Writer's Digest Books.

Dillard, A. (1989). *The writing life.* New York: HarperCollins.

Duckworth, E. (1996). *The having of wonderful ideas & other essays on teaching and learning, 2nd ed.* New York: Teachers College Press.

Edgerton, L. (2003). *Finding your voice: How to put personality in your writing.* Cincinnati, OH: Writer's Digest Books.

Failgley, L., & White, S. (1984). Measuring the effects of revisions on text structure. In R. Beach & L. Bridwell (Eds.), *New directions in composition research.* New York: Guilford Press.

Falk, B. (2000). *The heart of the matter: Using standards and assessment to learn.* Portsmouth, NH: Heinemann.

Fitzgerald, J. (1989). Enhancing two related thought processes: Revision in writing and critical reading. *Reading Teacher, 43,* 1.

Fitzgerald, J., & Markham, L. R. (1987). *Teaching children about revision in writing.* Paper presented at the annual meeting of the American Educational Research Association. Washington, DC.

Fletcher, R. (1993). *What a writer needs.* Portsmouth, NH: Heinemann.

Fletcher, R. (1996). *A writer's notebook: Unlocking the writer within you.* New York: Avon.

Fletcher, R., (1999). *Live writing: Breathing life into your words.* New York: Avon.

Fletcher, R. (2000). *How writers work: Finding a process that works for you.* New York: HarperCollins.

Fletcher, R., & Portalupi, J. (2001). *Nonfiction craft lessons: Teaching information writing K–8.* Portland, ME: Stenhouse.

Fletcher, R., & Portalupi, J. (1998). *Craft lessons: Teaching writing K–8.* York, ME: Stenhouse.

Fletcher, R. J., & Portalupi, J. (2001). *Writing workshop: The essential guide.* Portsmouth, NH: Heinemann.

Flynn, N., & McPhillips, S. (2000). *A note slipped under the door: Teaching from poems we love.* Portland, ME: Stenhouse.

Fountas, I. C., & Pinnell, G. S. (2001). *Guiding readers and writers grades 3–6: Teaching comprehension, genre, and content literacy.* Portsmouth, NH: Heinemann.

Fox, M. (1992). *Dear Mem Fox, I have read all your books even the pathetic ones: And other incidents in the life a children's book author.* New York: Harvest Books.

Fulwiler, T. (2003). A lesson in revision. In W. Bishop (Ed.), *The subject is writing.* Portsmouth, NH: Boynton/Cook.

Graves, D. (1983). *Writing: Teachers and children at work.* Portsmouth, NH: Heinemann.

Graves, D. H. (1994). *A fresh look at writing.* Portsmouth, NH: Heinemann.

Greenwood, S. C. (2004). *Words count: Effective vocabulary instruction in action.* Portsmouth, NH: Heinemann.

Hansen, J. (1991). *When writers read.* Portsmouth, NH: Heinemann.

Harwayne, S. (1992). *Lasting impressions: Weaving literature into the writing workshop.* Portsmouth, NH: Heinemann.

Harwayne, S. (1999). *Going public: Priorities & practices at the Manhattan New School.* Portsmouth, NH: Heinemann.

Harwayne, S. (2000). *Lifetime guarantees: Toward ambitious literacy teaching.* Portsmouth, NH: Heinemann.

Heard, G. (2003). *The revision toolbox: Teaching techniques that work.* Portsmouth, NH: Heinemann.

Horning, A. S. (2002). *Revision revisited.* Creskill, NJ: Hampton.

Horning, A. S. (2004). Revising research writing: A theory and some exercise. In W. Bishop (Ed.), *Acts of revision: A guide for writers.* Portsmouth, NH: Heinemann.

Iyer, P. (1996). In praise of the humble comma. In J. Kitchen & M. P. Jones (Eds.), *In short.* New York: W. W. Norton.

Jenkins, C. B. (1999). *The allure of authors: Author studies in the elementary classroom.* Portsmouth, NH: Heinemann.

Johnston, P. H. (2004). *Choice words: How our language affects children's learning.* Portland, ME: Stenhouse.

Koch, S. (2003). *The Modern Library's writing workshop.* New York: Random House.

Kotch, L., & Zackman, L. (1995). *Author studies in the elementary classroom.* New York: Scholastic.

Laminack, L., & Ray, K. W. (1996). *Spelling in use.* Urbana, IL: NCTE.

Lane, B. (1993). *After the end: Teaching and learning creative revision.* Portsmouth, NH: Heinemann.

Lattimer, H. (2003). *Thinking through genre: Units of study in reading and writing workshops, 4–12.* Portland, ME: Stenhouse.

Lee, A. (2000). *Composing critical pedagogies: Teaching writing as revision.* Urbana, IL: NCTE.

Morrison, T. (1998).Toni Morrison. In G. Plimpton (Ed.), *The Paris Review interviews: Women writers on their work.* New York: Modern Library.

Morrison, T. (1990). The pleasures of revision. In D. M. Murray (Ed.), *Shoptalk: Learning to write with writers.* Portsmouth, NH: Boynton/Cook.

Murray, D. (1995). *The craft of revision.* Fort Worth, TX: Harcourt Brace.

Murray, D. (1996). *Creating a life in essay, story, and poem.* Portsmouth, NH: Boynton/Cook.

Murray, D. M. (1985). *A writer teaches writing, 2nd ed.* Boston: Houghton Mifflin.

Murray, D. M. (1990). *Shoptalk: Learning to write with writers.* Portsmouth, NH: Boynton/Cook.

Murray, D. M. (1993). *Read to write, 3rd ed.* Fort Worth, TX: Harcourt Brace Jovanovich.

Murray, D. M. (1999). *Write to learn.* Fort Worth, TX: Harcourt Brace.

Nia, I. T. (1999). Units of study in the writing workshop. In *Primary Voices K–8. 8,* 1.

Nia, I. T. (in press). *Digging deeper.* Portsmouth, NH: Heinemann.

Noble, W. (1987). *"Shut up!" he explained: A writer's guide to the uses and misuses of dialogue.* Middlebury, VT: P. S. Eriksson.

Noble, W. (1994). *Conflict, action & suspense: How to pull readers in and carry them along with dramatic, powerful storytelling.* Cincinnati, OH: Writer's Digest Books.

Noden, H. R. (1999). *Image grammar: Using grammatical structures to teach writing.* Portsmouth, NH: Heinemann.

Oates, J. C. (2003). *The faith of a writer: Life, craft, art.* New York: HarperCollins.

Ozick, C. (1990). The pleasures of revision. In D. M. Murray (Ed.), *Shoptalk: Learning to write with writers.* Portsmouth, NH: Boynton/Cook.

Peck, R. (1992). Nobody but a reader ever became a writer. In D. R. Gallo (Ed.), *Authors' insights: Turning teenagers into readers & writers.* Portsmouth, NH: Boynton/Cook.

Peck, R. N. (1983). *Fiction is folks: How to create unforgettable characters.* Cincinnati, OH: Writer's Digest Books.

Peterson, R. (1992). *Life in a crowded place.* Portsmouth, NH: Heinemann.

Portalupi, J., & Fletcher, R. (2004). *Teaching the qualities of writing.* Portsmouth, NH: Heinemann.

Ramsey, A. (1981). *Rhetorical invention: Implications for rewriting.* Paper presented at the annual meeting of the Conference on College Composition and Communication. Dallas, TX.

Ray, K. W. (1999). *Wondrous words: Writers and writing in the elementary classroom.* Urbana, IL: NCTE.

Ray, K. W. (2001). *The writing workshop: Working through the hard parts (and they're all hard parts).* Urbana, IL: NCTE.

Ray, K. W. (2002). *What you know by heart: How to develop curriculum for your writing workshop.* Portsmouth, NH: Heinemann.

Reed, K. (1989). *Revision: How to find and fix what isn't working in your story and strengthen what is to build compelling, successful fiction.* Cincinnati, OH: Writer's Digest Books.

Romano, T. (1987). *Clearing the way: Working with teenage writers.* Portsmouth, NH: Heinemann.

Romano, T. (2004). *Crafting authentic voice.* Portsmouth, NH: Heinemann.

Rosenblatt, L. M. (1994). *The reader, the text, the poem: The transactional theory of the literary work.* Carbondale, IL: Southern Illinois University Press.

Routman, R. (1996). *Literacy at the crossroads.* Portsmouth, NH: Heinemann.

Schwartz, A. (1990). *Professional writers don't write like that, so why should you?* Paper presented at the annual meeting of the Conference on College Composition and Communication. Chicago, IL.

Shaughnessy, M. (1977). *Errors and expectations.* New York: Oxford University Press.

Snowball, D., & Bolton, F. (1999). *Spelling K–8: Planning and teaching.* York, ME: Stenhouse.

Spandel, V. (2001). *Creating writers through 6-trait writing assessment and instruction, 3rd ed.* New York: Addison Wesley Longman.

Stafford, W. E. (1994). *You must revise your life.* Ann Arbor, MI: University of Michigan Press.

Szczepanski, J. (2003). Hearing voices: Yours, mine and others. In W. Bishop (Ed.), *The subject is writing.* Portsmouth, NH: Boynton/Cook.

Truss, L. (2004). *Eats, shoots & leaves: The zero tolerance approach to punctuation.* New York: Gotham.

Vygotsky, L. (1986). *Thought and language.* Cambridge, MA: Massachusetts Institute of Technology Press.

Weaver, C. (1996). *Teaching grammar in context.* Portsmouth, NH: Boynton/Cook.

Weaver, C., McNally, C., & Moerman, S. (2001). To grammar or not to grammar: That is not the question! *Voices from the Middle,* (8)3, 17-33.

Welty, E. (1984). *One writer's beginnings.* Cambridge: Harvard University Press.

Zinsser, W. (1994). *On writing well, 5th ed.* New York: HarperCollins.

# Children's Books Cited

Baylor, B. (1978). *The other way to listen.* New York: Simon & Schuster.

Bunting, E. (1994). *A day's work.* New York: Clarion Books.

Bunting, E. (1991). *Fly away home.* New York: Clarion Books.

Bunting, E. (1996). *Going home.* New York: HarperCollins.

Bunting, E. (1994). *Smoky night.* San Diego: Harcourt Brace.

Bunting, E. (1993). *Someday a tree.* New York: Clarion.

Bunting, E. (2000). *Swan in love.* New York: Atheneum.

Coleman, E. (1996). *White socks only.* Morton Grove, IL: Albert Whitman.

Cooney, B. (1982). *Miss Rumphius.* New York: Viking Press.

Creech, S. (1994). *Walk two moons.* New York: HarperCollins.

DiCamillo, K. (2000). *Because of Winn-Dixie.* Cambridge, MA: Candlewick Press.

De Paola, T. (1978). *The clown of God.* New York: Harcourt.

Dragonwagon, C. (1990). *Home place.* New York: Macmillan.

Fleischman, S. (1986). *The whipping boy.* New York: Greenwillow.

Fletcher, R. (1998). *Flying solo.* New York: Random House.

Fox, M. (1989). *Night noises.* New York: Gulliver.

Fox, M. (1987). *Possum magic.* New York: Abington.

Fox, M. (1994). *Tough Boris.* New York: Harcourt.

Gray, L. M. (1993). *Dear Willie Rudd.* New York: Simon & Schuster.

Gray, L. M. (1995). *My mama had a dancing heart.* New York: Orchard.

Greenfield, E. (1992). *Grandpa's face.* New York: Putnam.

Henkes, K. (1986). *A weekend with Wendell.* New York: Greenwillow.

Henkes, K. (1991). *Chrysanthemum.* New York: Greenwillow.

Hesse, K. (1999). *Come on, rain!* New York: Scholastic.

Hesse, K. (1997). *Out of the dust.* New York: Scholastic.

Hesse, K. (2001). *Witness.* New York: Hyperion.

McCaughrean, G. (2002). *My grandmother's clock.* New York: Clarion.

Muth, J. J. (2002). *The three questions.* New York: Scholastic.

Napoli, D. J. (1997). *Stones in water.* New York: Dutton.

Paulsen, G. (1988). *Hatchet.* New York: Viking Penguin.

Polacco, P. (1994). *My rotten redheaded older brother.* New York: Simon & Schuster.

Polacco, P. (1998). *Thank you, Mr. Falker.* New York: Philomel.

Polacco, P. (1990). *Thunder cake.* New York: Philomel.

Ryan, P. M. (1998). *Riding freedom.* New York: Scholastic.

Rylant, C. (1992). *An angel for Solomon Singer.* New York: Orchard.

Rylant, C. (1999). *The cookie-store cat.* New York: Blue Sky Press.

Rylant, C. (1986). *Night in the country.* New York: Bradbury Press.

Rylant, C. (1985). *The relatives came.* New York: Bradbury Press.

Rylant, C. (1982). *When I was young in the mountains.* New York: Dutton.

Simon, S. (1993). *Wolves.* New York: HarperCollins.

Spinelli, J. (1996). *Crash.* New York: Knopf.

White, E. B. (1952). *Charlotte's web.* New York: Harper.

Woodson, J. (2001). *The other side.* New York: Putnam.

Woodson, J. (1997). *We had a picnic this Sunday past.* New York: Hyperion.

Yolen, J. (1997). *Miz Berlin walks.* New York: Philomel.

Zolotow, C. (1992). *The seashore book.* New York: HarperCollins.

# Index

## A

accomplishments, celebrating, 31-32

*After the End* (Lane), 179

Anderson, Carl, 43, 112

  *How's It Going?*, 64

Angelillo, Janet, *A Fresh Approach to Teaching Punctuation*, 125

assessing success, 177-178

  conferring with students and, 179-182

  mentor texts and, 185-187

  rubrics for, 178-179

  students' growth and, 183-185

assessment, initial, 34-38

  first unit of study, 39-40

attitudes toward revision, 23

audience, 117, 126

author studies, 67-69

  day-by-day teaching plan, 74-76

  planning, 70

  reading, writing concepts and, 69

  sample mentor, 70-74

  theories of, 72

  *See also* mentor authors

## B

Bambara, Toni Cade, 113

Bishop, Wendy, 26

Bolton, Faye, 30

books, professional, 27

Bunting, Eve, 74, 93

## C

Calkins, Lucy, 41, 43, 113, 130

Cambourne, Brian, 82-83

Carroll, Lewis, 10

character development, 94

"chunk"-level revisions, 135-137

Colangelo, Tina, 70-73

*Come On, Rain!* (Hesse), 123, 158

Condit, Amy, 181

conferences, writing, 43-44

conventions, 115, 125

*Cookie-Store Cat, The*, (Rylant), 168-169

*Craft Lessons* (Fletcher and Portalupi), 120

Creech, Sharon, *Walk Two Moons*, 141

Crichton, Michael, 189

Culham, Ruth, 40, 112, 126

  *6 + 1 Traits of Writing: The Complete Guide, Grades 3 and Up*, 112

## D

Daiute, C. A., 115

Daunis, Sarah, 94, 170-171

Dolan, Tina, 168

drafting techniques, 26

## E

*Eats, Shoots and Leaves* (Truss), 167

Edgerton, Lee, 115

editing, revision versus, 20

elaboration, 114, 120

elements of story, 79-81

  revision and, 82-83

encouragement, 25-26

## F

Falk, Beverly, 28

first unit of study

  assessing students for, 39-40

  carrying out, 44-53

  goals, general, 45

  introduction to revision in, 41

  revision strategies, 47-50

  topics, specific, 46-47

Fletcher, Ralph, 31, 112, 131-132

  *Craft Lessons*, 120

  *Flying Solo*, 58-63

  *Live Writing*, 21

  *Nonfiction Craft Lessons*, 107

  *What a Writer Needs*, 64

fluency, 115, 123-124

*Flying Solo* (Fletcher), 58-63

focus, 113, 117-119

Fox, Mem, 28, 114, 117

*Fresh Approach to Teaching Punctuation, A* (Angelillo), 125

## G

genre, 117, 127, 140, 155-157

grading, 179

grammar, 166, 171-175

*Grandpa's Face* (Greenfield), 146

Graves, Donald, 11, 24

Greenfield, Eloise, *Grandpa's Face*, 146

group, partner work, 28-29

## H

Heard, Georgia, 23

Heibert, Jacqueline, 97-102, 103-104

Henkes, Kevin, 70

  *Weekend with Wendell, A*, 71

Hesse, Karen, 76, 142-143

  *Come On, Rain!*, 123, 158

Hill, Laura, 98-102

Horning, Alice S., 23, 123

*How's It Going?* (Anderson), 64

## I

Iams, Maria, 180-181

independent inquiry, 161-164

"In Praise of the Humble Comma" (Iyer), 166

Iyer, Pico, "In Praise of the Humble Comma" 166

## K

Koch, Stephen, 145

Kotch, Laura, 67-68

## L

Lane, Barry, *After the End*, 179

Lehner, Mary Ellyn, 16-18

Levine, Phillip, 146-149

*Live Writing* (Fletcher), 21

## M

mentor authors, 65-67

  collecting texts of, 106, 185-187

  nonfiction writing and, 102

  realistic fiction writing, revision and, 89-90

  *See also* author studies

mentor sentences, punctuation and, 167-170

momentum, 142-143

Morrison, Toni, 11, 145, 189

Moscato, Kerry, 182

Murray, Donald, 15, 21, 31, 113, 117, 140

  *Write to Learn*, 64

## N

Nadler, Judy, 92, 185-187

Napoli, Donna Jones, *Stones in Water*, 170

*Night in the Country* (Rylant), 47-53, 121

*Nonfiction Craft Lessons* (Portalupi and Fletcher), 107

nonfiction writing

  day-by-day unit of study, 107-109

  editorials, 101

  feature articles, 101

  genres of, 99

  mentor authors and, 102